Aberdeenshire Library and Information Service
www.aberdeenshire.gov.uk/alis
Renewals Hotline 01224 661511

TAYLOR, David

Small pet handbook

TO BETTY AND ELIZABETH

First published in hardback in 1996 by
Collins, an imprint of
HarperCollins*Publishers*
77-85 Fulham Palace Road
Hammersmith, London W6 8JB

This paperback edition first published in 2002

The Collins website address is www.**collins**.co.uk

Collins is a registered trademark of HarperCollins Publishers Limited.

09 08 07 06 05 04 03
9 8 7 6 5 4 3 2

A catalogue record of this book is available from the British Library.

ISBN 0 00 713448 7

This book was created by SP Creative Design for HarperCollins*Publishers* Ltd
Editor: Heather Thomas
Designer: Rolando Ugolini
Illustrations: Al Rockall, Rolando Ugolini
Special photography: Animal Ark and Rolando Ugolini
Frank Lane Picture Agency: pages 8, 17, 80, 82, 84, 91, 93, 94
David Dalton: pages 66, 70

Acknowledgements
The publishers would like to thank the following for their kind assistance
in producing this book:
Scampers Petcare Superstore, Soham, Nr Ely, Cambs
Nicola and Thomas Atkinson

Colour reproduction by Colourscan, Singapore
Printed and bound by Printing Express Ltd, Hong Kong

small pet handbook

David Taylor
BVMS, FRCVS, FZS

Author

David Taylor, BVMS, FRCVS, FZS, is a well-known veterinary surgeon, broadcaster and author of over thirty books, including six volumes of autobiography, some of which formed the basis for three series of the BBC television drama *One by One*. The founder of the International Zoo Veterinary Group, he has exotic patients across the world, ranging from crocodiles to killer whales and giant pandas. He lives in Richmond, Surrey, with his wife, four cats and a hamster called 'Fudge'.

Contents

Introduction   **6**

CHAPTER ONE
Rabbits   **8**

CHAPTER TWO
Rodents   **24**

Guinea Pigs   **25**

Hamsters   **29**

Gerbils   **31**

Mice and rats   **34**

CHAPTER THREE
Acquiring your pet   **39**

CHAPTER FOUR
Food for the small pet   **68**

CHAPTER FIVE
Breeding   **81**

CHAPTER SIX
General care of your pet   **97**

CHAPTER SEVEN
When small pets fall ill   **103**

Index   **127**

Introduction

Small, as they say, is beautiful. That's certainly true of the small pets which are ideal for young folk, who are beginning to revel in the joys and responsibilities of animal-keeping, because of their relative cheapness to buy and maintain. However, they are also a fascinating hobby for innumerable adults. It is estimated that there are about 1.35 million rabbits, 730,000 hamsters and 610,000 guinea pigs in Britain at the present time, as well as tens of thousands of tame rats, mice and gerbils. Indeed, rabbits are the third most common pet examined by vets in their surgeries.

Although these small mammals generally cost less than dogs and cats, not to mention ponies and horses, they deserve and demand no less care and attention from their owners in order to ensure them long and happy lives. Such intriguing creatures are not to be regarded as children's toys, or down-market, disposable, second-rate pets. Housed and handled properly, and tended and treated with affection and interest, these little animals, which come in such a wide variety of breeds and colours, will provide limitless fascination, fun and, yes, friendship.

All of them are designed and constructed as intricately as dogs, horses or, indeed, human beings. Their delicate, complex anatomy and physiology, perfectly attuned to a particular mode of living on this planet, make man-made devices like computers and space rockets seem stone age by comparison. What's more, from a practical point of view, they are healthier to have around than, say, dogs or cats. Rabbits and rats and all the other small pets, in their domesticated forms, carry fewer diseases that can be transmitted to their owners than the bigger species.

To get the most out of your small pet means putting in a little effort to learn the do's and don'ts: the basic rules for maintaining them correctly. It isn't at all difficult as this little book will show you, and the more you learn about, observe and work with your pets, the more your enjoyment and delight will grow in these very special animals.

C H A P T E R   O N E

Rabbits

The name 'rabbit' probably comes from a mediaeval Dutch word 'robbe', which was originally a nickname for anyone called Robert.

■ Evolution of the rabbit

Rabbits are not rodents like rats, mice and other pets featured in this book, but are members of another group of mammals called lagomorphs. These creatures originated around 55,000,000 years ago and developed quite separately from the rodents. One key difference between rodents and lagomorphs is that whereas the former have only one pair of upper incisor (gnawing) teeth, the latter have two pairs. Modern scientific blood analysis shows the lagomorphs to be

These hares are 'boxing' in the mating season.

more closely related to hoofed animals than to rodents. There are
three main groups of lagomorphs:

■ Rabbits
■ Hares
■ Pikas

The last group, the pikas, is the least familiar to most of us. They
are small (1.25-2.5 cm/^{1}/$_2$-1 in long), with rounded ears, short legs
and virtually no tail. The only European species live in Russia. They
are hardy creatures of the mountains and one, the Tibetan pika,
can be found lying out in the Himalayan sun at altitudes above
5,500 m/18,000 ft and in temperatures of -15°C/5°F or less. The
main differences between rabbits and hares are outlined overleaf.

■ Rabbits in Britain

It is generally thought that rabbits were introduced into Britain
no earlier than 1066 when the Normans invaded. They brought
'warreners' with them – men who would stock and tend rabbit
warrens to supply the invaders' stomachs.

However, there is evidence that rabbits may have reached Britain
before the Normans. Fossilized remains record their presence before
the third Glacial Age (22,000 years ago). It is certain that they
didn't survive the icy conditions. After the ice receded, Europe and
North Africa were re-populated with rabbits moving out from the
Iberian Peninsula. Some scientists believe that rabbits may then
have crossed the land-bridge between France and Britain around
7000-6000 BC; England was connected to the Continent up to
about 5000 BC. It is also possible that the Romans, enthusiastic
trenchermen who had domesticated rabbits by the first century BC
and kept them in special walled enclosures called *leporia,* may have
introduced some of these animals.

Rabbit soon became a choice meat on mediaeval menus, and
their fur and skins were in demand. Rabbit embryos were considered
'meatless' and an acceptable food for fast days. By the fourteenth

Rabbits and hares

	Rabbits	Hares
At birth	Born naked, blind and helpless	Born well covered with fur and hop about shortly after birth
Nature	Generally gregarious	Generally solitary
Habitat	Usually in burrows	Usually above ground
Running	Scamper, no stamina	Excellent runners, good staying power

The best-selling book *Watership Down* helped to increase interest in rabbits and keeping them as pets.

century, rabbit was valued as highly as sucking pig. As agriculture evolved and natural predators, such as falcons and wild carnivores, diminished, rabbits became more of a problem to the farmers' crops. Trapping, snaring and ferreting continued with rabbits still popular for food and the furriery trade, but with three rabbits eating as much each day as one sheep, the loss of arable produce was significant by the nineteenth century.

Sending ferrets down the burrows to do battle with the rabbits underground had always been the most popular method of control, but all sorts of bizarre methods were tried to rid fields of the free-loading bunnies. Most interesting of all is the way in which farmers on the Isle of Wight fixed lighted candles to the backs of crabs and sent them down burrows, presumably to terrorize the rabbits into moving house. Crabs and lobsters were similarly employed in Devon and were known as 'sea ferrets'. And while all this was going on, gypsies in the Chilterns claimed to be getting even better results with 'ferreting' toads!

■ Species of rabbit

Wild rabbits occur in most but not all parts of the world. They
are absent from Scandinavia, the Balkans, Italy and Eastern Europe.
There are twenty-five species of wild rabbit worldwide, living in
a variety of habitats from the dense vegetation on the slopes of
volcanoes (the volcano rabbit) to bogs and swamps (the marsh
rabbit and swamp rabbit).

Only one Old World rabbit species exists: *Oryctolagus*. It covers
much of Europe and North Africa, was introduced into Australia and
New Zealand and elsewhere by settlers and is the origin of all
domestic rabbit breeds. Among the other twenty-four species is the
dark-coloured Pentalagus, found only on the Ryukyu Islands of Japan,

These handsome animals are English rabbits, a breed that
originated in the nineteenth century.

Names for rabbits

Countrymen had quaint names for different sorts of wild rabbit.

■ 'Warreners' lived in established warrens.

■ 'Parkers' were to be found in open country.

■ 'Hedgehogs' were those of thickly wooded areas or alternatively 'of no fixed abode'.

■ 'Sweethearts' were rabbits bred in captivity. Sweethearts of the eighteenth and nineteenth centuries were usually kept in pits and were fed on brewery grain, cabbage leaves, turnip tops and other vegetable refuse. Gradually, the selective breeding of the rabbit developed and by 1880 the keeping of rabbits as pets began to be very popular.

and the incredibly rare Nesolagus from Sumatra. This small rabbit with short ears and a mottled coat may already be extinct, as only thirteen specimens have ever been found!

■ European rabbits

The single species of European wild rabbit was and is found in a variety of different natural types. Albinos are rare, but a 'Dutch' marked variety with a white nose and saddle mark is not uncommon. A long-haired 'Angora' type lives on the Welsh islands of Skomer and Skokholm but rarely elsewhere, and melanistic (black) ones form almost a hundred per cent of the communities on the British Scilly Isles and the Islet of Samson.

By crossing and selecting from the fast and prolifically breeding animal, man 'produced' the fifty-odd breeds and around eighty varieties of the modern rabbit fancy. You can choose from a wide range of sizes, coat colours, designs and textures. With the glamorous varieties of domesticated pet rabbit now available we are a long way from Watership Down.

■ Domesticated rabbits

There are four main groups of domesticated rabbit:

■ Normal fur

These include Chinchilla, Havana, New Zealand, Sable, Smoke Pearl, Fox, Lilac and Chinchilla giganta. Some Normal Furs, such as the Squirrel, Glavcot and Perle de Hal, are now extinct. The breeds come in a variety of elegant colours.

■ Rex

These breeds have a plush coat, about 1.25 cm/^{1}/$_2$ in long and with a velvety touch. They include the Self, Shaded and Tan. Again, there are lots of named colour varieties.

■ Satins

Here the fur is shiny to the touch due to each hair being flattened and with little or no hollow centre. The breeds of Satin come

There are many breeds of rabbit, and they come in a wide range of colours and sizes, such as the Dutch rabbits (top) and Old English (above), which are among the fancy breeds.

Coneys

Incidentally, the coney mentioned in the Bible is not the rabbit. The word 'coney' does indeed come from the Latin for rabbit and it is still used to mean rabbit in heraldry and the fur-trade. Many dictionaries and biblical scholars confuse the two words, but the conies that 'are but a feeble folk, yet make they their houses in the rocks' (Proverbs) refers to a totally different rodent-like creature (actually the closest living relative of the elephant) called the Syrian hyrax which lives in Palestine.

in a broad spectrum of colours with names like Argent, Fox, Himalayan, Ivory, Lilac, Marten Sable, Opal and Smoke Pearl.

■ Fancy breeds

These include the Angora, Belgian Hare, Dutch, English, Harlequin Magpie, Himalayan, Lop, Netherland Dwarf, Polish, Silver and Tan. **Note:** There are well-known breeds like that schoolboy's favourite, the Dutch, and real rarities such as the Orange-buff Shaded Rex and the Smoke Pearl Marten Rex. No rabbit could be humble with names like these.

■ Weight

Lagomorphs range in weight from 100 grams ($3^1/_2$ oz) for the smallest pikas up to around 4.6 kg (over 10 lb) for the largest wild hares. Domestic breeds of rabbit can exceed that with weights of 5.5 – 6.3 kg (12 – $13^3/_4$ lb), generally in adult Flemish Giants; the record is 11.3 kg (almost 25 lb), achieved by both a Flemish Giant and a Norfolk Star. It must be admitted, however, that rabbits are not particularly efficient users of food. The rate at which they extract available energy from foodstuffs is only about one-third of that achieved by sheep or cows. However, they are more 'damp-resistant' than sheep, and they have survived in wet, chilly environments that have wiped out sheep flocks.

■ Voice

Rabbits are not, usually, very noisy creatures. They are generally non-vocal unless injured or frightened, although some do give little grunts of pleasure. One species, the South African red 'hare' (*Pronolagus*), emits a high-pitched warning call when trouble is brewing.

■ Speed

Unlike the hare, which can clock up to 80 kmph/50 mph, the rabbit is not a very fast runner. It dashes and scampers and seeks the safety of a burrow rather than trying to outrun a pursuer. It is, however,

quite an accomplished swimmer, and the marsh and swamp rabbits (*Sylvilagus* species) of the Americas and the West Indies take to water with gay abandon. Surprisingly, rabbits also climb well and can be found living in the thatched roofs of cottages in the Hebrides. The rabbit's foot has hair on the under-surface to afford a good grip.

■ Vision

Rabbits possess good eyesight but are colour-blind. The most impressive aspect is their range of vision. With eyes set well out on both sides of the head, they cover a field of over 300° – they can literally see behind them. The eyes can move in conjunction or independently of each other. Because of the position of their eyes, rabbits do not see stereoscopically, as do men and monkeys for example, but to hunted animals stereoscopic vision is less important than all-round warning capability.

Other creatures that usually find themselves playing the part of innocent victims, e.g. the mouse, shrew and partridge, also have eyes set to the sides like the rabbit. The problem is the area in front of the nose, particularly the nearest 2 m/6 ft, which is poorly seen by the rabbit or hare. To overcome this difficulty, it has to tip its head a little to one side so that one eye at a time can scan the awkward zone.

The position of the eyes explains why, when a hare is pursued by a dog, it lifts its head up and lays its ears back: it can see the dog behind. But it has that blind spot dead ahead and in full flight there's no time to mess about tipping one's head to right or left. Consequently, hares sometimes dash headlong over a cliff or straight into a pair of human legs.

There is no shimmering, reflecting mirror behind the retina of a rabbit as seen in a hunter, such as the cat. The red colour of an albino's eyes is simply the layer of blood vessels behind the retina. There is also, however, an intriguing dull eyeshine frequently seen in rabbits; scientists do not understand how this is produced. The retina, the light-sensitive 'film' of the eye, is much more highly organised and complex in rabbits than in man or other primates. Whereas the rabbit sorts out and interprets in the retina itself much of the visual information coming into the eye, higher creatures, such as primates, have shifted such functions back into the more sophisticated sight-control areas of the brain. The poor rabbit needs what little brain he's got for other things.

■ Smell

Rabbits are excellent sniffers; they're so good that they go hunting the elusive underground truffle fungus by scent alone. All that nose-twitching of rabbits and hares is probably linked with smell, but there

Scent

This is very important to rabbits. Males use odours to mark out their territory and their possessions. They do this either by spraying urine (with considerable accuracy and range) or by transferring a special substance from glands under their chins on to their paws and then stamping it along their boundary lines or rubbing it on to females and young belonging to them. Chin-scratching in rabbits denotes male chauvinism rather than an irritating itch.

may be some additional sensory function extracting information from the air. Beneath the twitching folds of skin but in front of the nostrils are two hairless patches of skin in the form of oval, raised pads covered with pimples and ridges. What do they detect? How do they work? Science has yet to find out. Rabbits are by no means smelly creatures. Young rabbits are remarkably free of scent and necessarily so in a world of keen-nosed predators. A fox, which can locate eggs buried 10 cm/4 in deep when passing by at a distance 2.7 m/3 yd, normally misses baby rabbits buried in sand by their mother while she goes out searching for food.

■ Hearing and taste

Rabbits come fully equipped with other highly developed senses. Hearing is first-class with long, mobile ear flaps, which can swivel about to scoop faint sounds out of the air. As befits such a vegetarian epicure, the rabbit appears to enjoy a sense of taste which is likewise one of the best around. The rabbit mouth possesses 17,000 taste buds compared with only 10,000 in man, only 400 in parrots and a minute 30-60 in pigeons.

■ Teeth and digestion

Rabbit teeth are not at all like ours or those of the dog or cat. They keep on growing continually throughout life, pushing continually up out of the gum and being worn down to convenient size by chewing.

Rabbit bowels are notable mainly for the presence of a well-developed large intestine where the fibrous vegetable food is acted

Touch

Like other animals with whiskers, the rabbit uses these sensitive touch-antennae, particularly at night. The whiskers also feel for the walls of the familiar dark tunnels under the ground, and the feel of the home burrow is registered in the kinaesthetic (touch) memory section of the brain. Put a rabbit in a strange burrow and the alarm bells begin ringing in this programmed memory bank; under such conditions a rabbit is likely to panic. So unpleasant is the idea of a foreign burrow to a rabbit that it will usually seek any sort of refuge (bushes, reeds etc), even with a hunter hot on its heels, rather than use a handy foreign hole.

on by the population of digestive microbes. This microbial digestion is similar to what happens in the stomachs of cud-chewing animals, such as cows, and when the germs have done their work the contents of the intestine are much richer in useful nourishment. Unfortunately, quite a lot of this potentially useful digested food passes out of the body in the droppings. Very sensibly the rabbit, true to the maxim 'waste not, want not', eats these droppings and thereby gets the benefit of the vitamins and other goodies that it nearly lost. This dropping-eating process is called 'refection'. It only applies to softer, light-coloured stools, which in wild rabbits are usually passed when they are resting in

their burrows. The darker, drier droppings passed when the rabbit is out and about contain much less nourishment and are not eaten.

The two types of dropping are easily recognised in domestic rabbits, although some pets are so quick at eating the more delectable variety that you may miss seeing them. Rabbits and hares, of course, are not ruminants like cattle, sheep, deer and antelopes; in other words, they don't chew cud.

■ Fur

Every rabbit comes with an excellent fur coat, which is composed in most breeds of long 'guard' hairs and undercoat. Moulting takes place normally once a year and spreads backwards from the front of the shoulders, over the flanks, and ends finally with the underbelly. The 'guard' hairs are absent in Rex rabbits but luxuriously long in Angoras.

■ Coat colour and lifespan

Some domestic rabbits produce different coat colours depending upon the temperature at which they are kept. Himalayans, for example, are pure white in an environment above 28°C/84°F.

These white Lops have a soft coat with long 'guard' hairs.

At lower temperatures, they show black paws, black tips to the ears and black saddlemarks. The low temperatures for some reason stimulate the production of black pigment cells in the skin while the hair is growing. The rabbit's lifespan is normally six to eight years.

This Old English rabbit has a distinctive coat.

CHAPTER TWO

Rodents

Apart from the rabbit, the other small pets in this book are all rodents. Rodents, which are characterized by having one pair of upper and one pair of lower incisor teeth designed for gnawing, are the most numerous of all mammals (fifty per cent of all species of mammal fall into the Order *Rodentia*).

■ Size

They range in size from the Old World harvest mouse, which can weigh as little as 4.2 grams (one-seventh of an ounce), up to the South American capybara which tips the scales at 30-50 kg/65-110 lb. Fossil rodents as big as wild boar and with heads the size of bulls have been discovered in Uruguay.

Guinea pigs (or cavies)

All of these mini-pets, as we have noted, are equipped with nipping incisor teeth, and a hamster, if provoked or neglected, can bite painfully. Yet none is more gentle and uncomplaining than our next subject, the cavy, commonly called the guinea pig.

Where does the strange name come from? The animal itself originated in South America, where wild relatives are still to be found in Peru. Some guinea pigs live at very high altitudes in the mountains. Scarcity of meat animals in the Andes led the pre-Inca natives to domesticate the guinea pig. Indeed, for centuries it was the only domesticated food animal of Peru, and it was also used as a sacrifice to the gods. Guinea pigs began to spread out of the Inca empire following the Spanish conquests of the mid-sixteenth century, and arrived in Europe via West Africa (by way of Guinea, perhaps?) in the seventeenth century. However, the word 'Guinea' may not have

The English guinea pig is the most popular variety.

In the wild

Whatever the origin of these animals' odd name, they are admirable individuals. In the wild, they live peaceably in burrows, mess about a bit in the day and a bit at night, being neither strictly nocturnal nor strictly diurnal, eat a purely vegetarian diet and converse with one another in faint squeaks and grunts.

any geographical significance. In the seventeenth and eighteenth centuries it meant 'foreign' or 'strange'.

■ Varieties

There are three main varieties of domestic guinea pig:
- ■ The English (commonest)
- ■ The Abyssinian
- ■ The Peruvian (least common)

■ **The English variety** is short-haired and comes in self-coloured types (cream, black, white, agouti etc.) or as mixtures of two colours ('bicolours') or three colours ('tricolours'). Colour patterns similar to those in rabbits are given the same names (e.g. Himalayan, Dutch etc.).

■ **Abyssinians** are also short-coated but the coat is rougher and arranged in whorls and rosettes. This variety also comes in many different colours.

■ **The Peruvian** is long-haired (hairs up to 2 cm/^{3}/$_4$ in long) and again is to be found in various colours.

■ Vision and lifespan

Unlike hamsters, and most other rodents, guinea pigs do have some degree of colour vision. Their average lifespan is four to eight years.

■ Teeth, gnawing and chewing

Guinea pigs are typical rodents. They have the four characteristic, chisel-like incisor teeth, which continue to grow throughout the entire lifetime of the animal. When gnawing, there is a forward and backwards movement of the lower incisors which bite against the upper pair. While this is going on the grinding cheek teeth or molars do not meet one another, and indeed the back of the mouth can be shut off by pulling in the cheeks behind the incisors. This mechanism allows gnawing to proceed for some time without swallowing gnawed material and saves wear on the molars. When the guinea pig decides to change from gnawing to chewing, the lower jaw moves backwards, one set of incisors fits neatly behind the other, and the molars come into contact to begin the grinding process prior to swallowing. All this fancy mouth-work is controlled by a complicated set of special muscles.

Digestion

Again, like other rodents, guinea pigs possess a large caecum, a cul-de-sac lying at the junction between the small and large intestines where vegetable matter (often full of cellulose and tough to break down) can spend some time for digestion to be completely effective.

Hamsters

These stout Old World rodents include such species as the tiny
Chinese hamster and the European or black-bellied hamster as well as
the golden hamster, the commonest one found in the petshops. In
the wild, these solitary animals live in burrows and feed on fruit, grain
and vegetables. Some species eat insects and other small creatures.
All hamsters possess cheek-pouches into which they can pack food,
and hence their name. It comes from German, where 'hamster'
means 'hoarder'.

■ Colour, weight and sight

Over thirty colour varieties of golden hamster have been produced by
selective breeding. These include cream, cinnamon, white sepia,
honey, silver-blue and dark, normal and light golden. They can be

Golden hamsters

The golden hamster is sometimes called the Syrian hamster
although, in fact, the species is not confined to Syria but is
native to the steppes of Asia Minor and the Balkans. Every single
hamster in captivity today is descended from a single family of
golden hamsters which was captured in Syria by Dr Aharoni in
1932. They were taken to the Hebrew University of Jerusalem
and were found to thrive well. The family consisted of a female
and seven young. Four escaped and one female was killed by a
male. That left one male and two females. These three animals
formed the ancestral stock of almost every golden hamster that
has ever been kept in a laboratory or a youngster's bedroom
despite a further introduction of wild stock made in 1971. They
bred well and were first exported to the United States in 1938.
So much for the dangers of in-breeding!

banded. There are also piebalds, mosaics, satinized and tortoiseshells. Their eyes may be black, red or ruby in colour.

The basic golden hamster is reddish-brown in colour with white underparts, measures 15-20 cm/6-8 in long and weighs 85-130 g/ 3-5 oz. It is colour-blind and sees the world in black and white.

■ Development and activity

Anatomically, hamsters are constructed to a design that is basically the same as that of the rabbit or mouse. Biologically the most striking thing about them is their remarkably rapid rate of development. A hamster takes only sixty days to proceed from being a single egg-cell in its mother's uterus to becoming a parent itself.

Hamsters are mainly active in the darker hours, particularly between 8 and 11 pm, and if the dark and light periods of the day are reversed artificially, they adjust their activity to the times when the lights are low. During their daily 'busy' time, they may regularly travel between eleven and twenty-one kilometres. In captivity, their energy is directed particularly towards escaping, and females in heat generally show an ingenious determination to go absent without leave. Hamsters are very fastidious animals much given to grooming, especially after being touched by human hands. Their normal life expectancy is one to three years.

Regular gentle handling is good for hamsters.

Gerbils

The friendly, inquisitive gerbil, with its brownish (agouti) fur and large dark eyes, is a very popular pet. The usual species found in a pet shop is the Mongolian gerbil, but sometimes you will come across the Libyan kind. In fact, over eighty species of gerbil exist, and they differ widely in size, colour, length of tail and even the colour of their toe nails. Pet gerbils have now been bred in other colours besides brown. There are also albinos, blacks and piebalds.

■ In the wild

Gerbils are rodents which are particularly adapted to arid environments: they are found in the wild in the deserts and steppes of Africa and Asia, and from the south-west of Russia in the west to the north of China in the east.

Most gerbils spend their days in underground burrows where the temperature is constant at about 20-25°C/68-79°F, sometimes blocking the entrance to their hidey-hole with a stone or lump of earth. High temperatures can be quickly lethal to these little animals and most species are nocturnal, venturing out to forage for food in the cool of the night. Mongolian and Great gerbils of the colder, northern lands are among the few species that are active by day and night.

■ Digestion

Obtaining and conserving water is crucially important to gerbils. They obtain some by 'burning' the carbohydrates in the seeds and other vegetable matter that they eat, but they also collect such food when it is damp with dew. Their digestive system extracts water from the food with great efficiency, allowing them to pass very dry droppings, and their powerful kidneys retain as much water as possible so that they produce only a few drops of very concentrated urine.

Although most gerbils are herbivorous, they will eat almost anything else they find. One species, Wagner's gerbil, has a passion for snails.

Pet gerbils

Pet gerbils tame quickly, seldom bite and have a life expectancy of around two years. Good jumpers, they nevertheless have no idea of heights and so should not be left alone on a table as they may well leap off and injure themselves.

Survival in the wild

Gerbils' bodies are modified specially in ways that aid survival when predators are about.

■ They possess very large middle ears enabling them to detect the soft wing beats of owls.

■ Their eyes are set so as to provide a wide field of vision.

■ For camouflage, their coat colours are the same as that of the terrain on and in which they live. Even within the same species, gerbils living among dark brown volcanic rocks develop dark brown fur while those living in orange sand have orange fur.

■ The long tail acts as a stabilizer when jumping and as a support when standing on the hind legs to look around.

The pale-coloured underparts of the gerbil reflect heat from the hot ground of the desert and thus help cool the animal.

Mice and rats

Now we come to the smallest and most inexpensive subjects of this book, traditionally beloved by small boys and looked at askance by most elderly folk above the age of fifteen. Small they may be and easy on the pocket (and in the pocket of many a young enthusiast), but they are pieces of biological engineering as intricate and intriguing as any of the more high-falutin' pets.

Lively, easily tamed, loving little individuals, tame breeds of rat are clean, gentle, fascinating creatures that carry less risk of disease for their owners than domestic dogs. They 'bond' with humans more easily than any other kind of small pet, and tame mice are neither Robert Burn's 'wee sleekit, cow'rin', tim'rous beasties' nor voracious little demons.

■ Varieties of mouse

As a group, mice are a varied and enterprising bunch and are by no means limited to holes in skirting boards, lumps of cheese and sinking ships. There are the birch mice of Eurasia that leap rather than run, live in burrows and sensibly hibernate in the bitter winters of the steppes; the grasshopper mice of North America that share burrows with prairie dogs and are useful in controlling insects, their favourite food, and sometimes kill birds or other rodents; the jumping mice with grey, golden or yellow-brown fur, long hind legs and very long tails, some of which live in America while other little-known ones roam the Giant Panda forests of China; and the spiny pocket mice of the Mexican deserts with their harsh fur.

Species of mice and rats

There are dozens of different wild mouse and rat species, and
the domesticated ones come in a wide variety of colours and
patterns, not just 'school boy white'. Both rats and mice can be
bi-coloured. Hooded rats are bi-coloured with one of the
colours covering the head and shoulders to resemble a hood.

Russia has the delicate Selevin's mouse, a stout little fellow only
discovered in 1939. It loves to scoff spiders and is very nocturnal;
in fact, it can't take more than a few minutes of sunshine without
becoming ill! Between Alaska and the tip of South America live over
sixty species of deer mice, pretty creatures with big eyes, fur that can
range in colour from white through brown to black but always with
'spatted' white feet. In Australia, sure enough, there's a mouse with a

pouch, the marsupial mouse, which is not a true mouse at all but a diminutive relative of the kangaroo. These are just a few of the many different species in existence.

■ Types of rat

What is the difference between a rat and a mouse? Not an easy question; it isn't a question of size for there are small species of rat and large species of mouse. To scientists, rats and mice are simply names given to various species within the animal family Muridae. Rats have more rows of scales on their tails (210 or more) than do mice (never more than 180).

Apart from the notorious brown rat and the black rat, there are water rats with large, laterally compressed tails which are used for sculling, swamp rats, tree rats, field rats, jerboa rats, bamboo rats and kangaroo rats to name but a few. Jerboa rats have long hind limbs and tufted tails and are found in North Australia. Africa has giant rats measuring two and a half feet in total length, the spiny tree rat with its spiny coat and Rhabdomys, the field rat with four stripes. In the Solomon Islands you will find a woolly rat, Capromys, whereas New Guinea is the home of Mallomys, a very large species with gorgeous long hair speckled with white, and Anisomys, which is coarse-haired

and creamy-coloured all over except for a dark base to its tail. The
rarest rodent in the world is probably Swarth's rice rat. Only four
have ever been seen alive (in 1906), and it wasn't recorded again
until 1966 when the skull of a recently dead animal was found.
The home of this elusive creature, if it still exists, is on James Island
in the Galapagos.

Our elegant, well-bred tame rats might well frown on the black
sheep of the rodent family, their infamous cousins the wild black and
brown rats. There are estimated to be around a hundred million of
these two species in the United States, and each animal costs the
country hundreds of millions of dollars per year in crop spoilage alone.

■ Life expectancy and sight

The life expectancy of the average rat or mouse in the wild is
generally short and can be reckoned in weeks or months. Pet mice,
however, will reach three years and sometimes five years. They have
in-built (possibly truly magnetic) homing instincts but are almost
certainly colour-blind, viewing their world only in black and white.

■ Water requirements

Like most rodents, mice and rats need to take in little water; they
produce almost all they require under normal circumstances by
'burning' the carbohydrates in the food they eat and using the water

Adaptation to environment

Being versatile and generally not over-specialized, rats and mice
have successfully adapted to nearly every environment the
Earth has to offer. For example, house mice sometimes live
inside the insulating material within refrigerator walls and adapt
to the chillier lifestyle by growing longer hair.

that is released in their bodies as a by-product of the 'burning'. This metabolic water is produced by larger animals, including man, but to them it is a minor source of H_2O; their relatively massive bodies demand far more water than such an internal spring can supply. Desert species, such as the spiny mouse, like the gerbils, can survive happily without any external source of water. As an extra water conservation measure, such species produce only limited amounts of droppings and a highly concentrated urine. Some spiny mice can live purely on tiny quantities of sea-water and even your ordinary house mouse can get by almost indefinitely without liquids. However, this does not mean that you should ever leave your tame rats and mice without a source of fresh, clean water! They are domesticated varieties which, particularly in the case of rats, may not be as hardy as their wild cousins.

Agility and movement

Some species, such as the kangaroo rats and jumping mice, are excellent jumpers; they have very enlarged tympanic bullae (the bony covering of the middle ear) which are concerned with balancing and also, possibly, with improving hearing in the desert where these creatures live.

South American fish-eating rats and water rats are naturally first-class swimmers. Some are skilled climbers, like the tree rats and tree mice. The wild black rat is a fine climber, being originally a tree-dweller, and it can dash along telephone wires more nimbly than any tight-rope walker. Although many naturalists believe that the brown rat cannot climb, this is untrue; it is not as agile as its black rat relative but it can clamber up things quite proficiently.

CHAPTER THREE

Acquiring your pet

So you think a pet rabbit, guinea pig, hamster, gerbil, rat or mouse is just the thing for you. But wait, are you just the thing for a pet? Before taking on the responsibility of owning any sort of living, breathing, feeling creature, there are some points that you should consider carefully. Ask yourself the following questions and answer them honestly.

1 Are you committed enough to look after the animal or animals for 365 days a year, not just for the first week or two before the novelty wears off?

2 What about holidays – what then?

3 Do you know about the animals' needs for housing, exercise, feeding etc?

4 Will you be able to provide enough space for animals that love company like rabbits and guinea pigs?

5 Do you know whether they smell and can you, day in, day out, combat all odours by regular cleaning, replacement of bedding and general hygienic measures?

6 How long do you expect your pet to live?

7 Are there any dogs or cats in the household which might taken an unhealthy interest in such smaller pets?

8 Do you know where, apart from this book, to obtain information on the successful keeping of the animals you have in mind?

Getting ready for your pet

If you can answer all the above points satisfactorily then the next
stage is to assemble the housing and accessories for your pet (see
page 49). Everything must be ready and in place before you bring
the new animal/s home. When it is all prepared, small pets can be
obtained from several sources.

■ Pet shops

Nowadays there are many excellent pet shops. You should frequent
the sort that are obviously well-run with sparkling, clean spacious
cages for the animals on sale and staff who gladly answer any
questions you may have. If you have any doubts concerning matters
of health, speak to your veterinary surgeon before making a purchase.

■ Hobbyists and breeders

Other sources of small pets, particularly the fancy breeds, are
hobbyists and breeders. You can find the latter in clubs and societies
or in the advertisement columns of specialist magazines and
periodicals, such as *Exchange and Mart*.

Good, clean
quarters are
essential for a
healthy pet.

Handling your pet

When selecting your pet you will certainly want to handle it and to
do so correctly. Here is some useful advice.

■ Rabbits

Rabbits are easily frightened and must be handled with care. If badly
handled, they can struggle violently and may injure their spinal cords,
perhaps seriously. Severe fear and stress can induce a fatal heart
attack in any small pet.

⚠ **Warning:** never pick a rabbit up by its ears. If it is nervous or
fractious, grasp the scruff with one hand and support the
rump with the palm of your other hand. Tamer rabbits may not like
the indignity of being 'scruffed'. With such an individual, put one
hand under the chest, holding each foreleg separately between the
thumb and two fingers,
and, as above, take the
weight with your other
hand under the rump.
When carrying a rabbit
thus held, keep it close to
your chest. The animal is
then best placed on a
solid non-slip surface,
such as a table, but still
restrained by your hands.

This shows the
correct way to hold a
nervous rabbit –
gently but firmly.

■ Guinea pigs

Gently but firmly grasp the animal round its shoulders, lift it up and then support the rump with your other hand.

■ Hamsters

They can be handled like guinea pigs or, if grumpy, can be scruffed, although you should remember that the scruff of a guinea pig can be rather large and slack because of the animal's extensive elastic cheek pouches.

Firm but very gentle handling is essential for guinea pigs.

■ Gerbils

Never pick a gerbil up by its tail – the skin may peel off! Support it on
the palm of one hand and hold the base of the tail between finger and
thumb of the other hand to stop it leaping off, perhaps disastrously.
It can also be gently 'scruffed' and pressed down against the palm
if extra restraint is required, but should never be lifted by the scruff.

Warning: gerbils may panic if they are restrained on their
backs – don't do it.

■ Rats and mice

■ Rats can be grasped around their shoulders (with your thumb
beneath the lower jaw if they are frightened and likely to bite).
Nervous rats can be briefly lifted by the base of their tails.

Warning: they should never be 'scruffed'.

■ Mice can be lifted briefly by their tails and then gently 'scruffed'
by the other hand. Frequent, gentle, firm handling keeps your pet
tame and amenable.

Warning: frightened mice and rats can bite.

Handle gerbils
and hamsters
carefully to
avoid falls.

What to look for when selecting your pet

■ Rabbits

If you're a beginner or if it is to be a child's first rabbit, a Dutch rabbit, Himalayan, Netherland Dwarf or (long-eared) Lop would fill the bill admirably. All of these breeds are known for their docility. Inspect your rabbit for signs of good health.

The coat should be clean, in good condition and with signs of self-grooming.

Look at the hindquarters for signs of dirty, smeared fur, which indicates diarrhoea.

The animal should be perky and fussing around, nose atwitch, when outside its nest.

Warning: take care with a strange rabbit. It may bite, and it can be a hard, painful bite at that!

The ears must be clean and empty of crusts, cheesy matter or unpleasant smelling stuff.

There must be no signs of 'matter' or excessive water discharge from the eyes or nose.

Breathing should be regular, silent and at a rate of between thirty-five and sixty-five breaths per minute (up to a hundred per minute for babies).

Always have a look at the prominent incisor teeth; they should be evenly balanced and not so overgrown that they nip the skin of the lips.

Look out for discolouration of the fur of the fore-paws which will accompany persistent rubbing of an irritated or inflamed nose.

■ Guinea pigs

Points to watch out for when buying a guinea pig are as follows:

There must be no discharge from eyes, ears, nose or mouth.

The coat should be dense without being coarse.

An alert animal with a shiny coat which is unsoiled by droppings or urine.

The breathing should be regular and silent.

When handled, the animal should feel 'solid' and well covered.

Droppings should be formed without evidence of diarrhoea.

■ Hamsters

It is always best to buy only young hamsters. The animal you
choose should inspect you as closely as you inspect it. This
hamster is exactly the sort of pernickety pet that you require.

Look for an immature animal
that is 7.5-10 cm (3-4 in) long
with wide-open, beady eyes.

It should have an
alert, inquisitive
manner and not be
alarmed by handling.

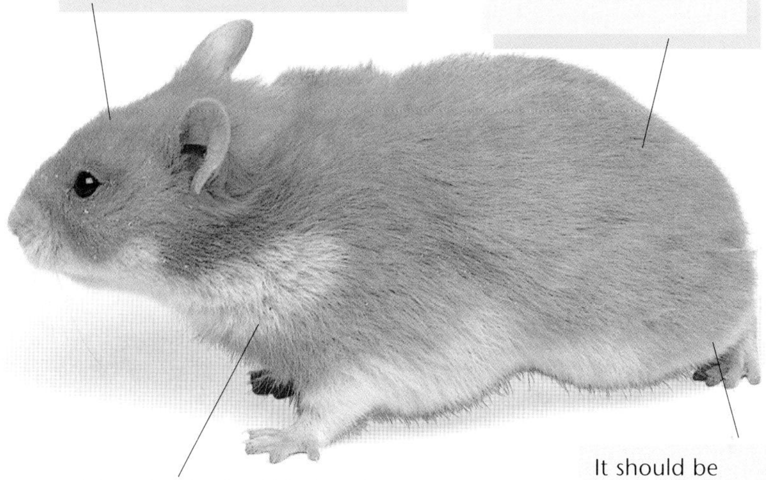

The fur should be smooth
and unbroken.

It should be
utterly clean in
appearance.

Note: make allowances, of course, for a hamster disturbed while
napping during the daytime. Hamsters are grumpy and lethargic
for a while if rudely awakened and are therefore perhaps best
inspected late in the day.

■ Gerbils, rats and mice

An acceptable gerbil, mouse or rat should be very much of a busybody, always on the go and verging on the nosey. Look for the following points:

The eyes, ears, nose, mouth and rear end should be clean and clear.

The animal must be neither too thin nor too fat. Mice that are plump may well be one year old or more and thus 'senior citizens'.

Tails must be intact, smooth-skinned or, in the case of gerbils, smooth-furred and completely unblemished.

It should not resent gentle handling and should be quite easy to catch.

There must be no sign of lameness when moving about.

The fur should be sleek and not 'staring', without any thin or bald spots.

Housing your pets

There are so many designs of housing for small pets available in pet shops. However, some are too small or too flimsily built, so if you have any doubts it may be best to have the housing, particularly for rabbits, built to your specifications. Finding suitable accommodation 'off the peg' can also sometimes be difficult in the case of pet rats. To help you make choices that will give your pet a high quality of life, I give you the basic requirements overleaf.

Spacious, dry, draught-proof hutches must be positioned correctly, preferably in the shade and not facing into the sun or wind.

Rabbits

Puffins on Puffin Island, off Anglesey, cheekily evict rabbits from their burrows during the nesting season, taking over and 'squatting' in the holes until the chicks are reared! They are intent on keeping the rabbits out, but the difficulty of keeping rabbits in led to the use of rabbit islands in the olden days. Queen Elizabeth I of England established several such water-surrounded collections to supply her kitchens.

The pet-owner nowadays hardly needs to go to such lengths. Hutches and runs are economical in space and cheap to set up. No back garden or yard is too small for a suitable and satisfactory set-up for one or two rabbits. These excellent pets are truly energy-saving, being essentially self-exercising (unlike the dog) and simple to house (unlike the pony).

■ Housing a rabbit

A hutch for, say, two medium-sized does (male rabbits often fight if housed together, and does and bucks are best housed separately), should be well built of strong timber at least 15 mm/^{1}/$_2$ in thick.

■ The dimensions should be no less than 150 x 60 x 60 cm/60 x 24 x 24 in, with two compartments, the living room and the bedroom or nest box.

■ There should be a pitched roof sloping backwards and with an overhang at the front covered with a tough waterproof material.

A hutch should be divided into two: the living area and the nest box.

Temperature range

Rabbits prefer a temperature range of 10°-18°C/47-64°F, but are very hardy outside these limits. However, you should beware of temperatures above 28°C/84°F: when it becomes that hot there is a strong risk of heat exhaustion with possibly fatal results. Should the thermometer climb above 28°C/84°F, hose down the hutch with cold water or release the rabbit into the cooler parts of the garden.

■ There should be a strong wire mesh front to one side of the living room, about 80 cm/32 in high.

■ The hutch should have legs to raise it from the ground.

■ Always allow enough room for the animals to grow.

■ The interior should be given a smooth finish – I prefer Formica.

■ The nest box must be big enough to allow the rabbits to stretch out on their sides.

■ The solid floor should be protected either by coating with polyurethane to make it watertight, or provided with a shallow galvanized tray containing a 5-cm/2-in deep layer of litter (softwood shavings or sawdust fit the bill).

■ Wire mesh floors are undesirable – they reduce cleaning, of course, but stop animals eating their valuable night droppings.

■ Any wood preservatives used must be non-toxic.

■ Hay or straw should be provided in the sleeping compartment, which is fitted with a draught-proof solid door. Side doors are far better than hatches in the roof or removable roofs. In the wild, predators tend to seize rabbits from above and, instinctively, domestic rabbits can be alarmed by hands approaching suddenly from on high.

■ A wooden panel with ventilation holes or a curtain of thick sacking should be attachable in front of the living room mesh for use in conditions of driving rain, extreme cold etc.

Exercise runs must be moved frequently on to fresh grass.

■ Positioning the hutch

The best direction for positioning the hutch is towards the south-east, not facing directly into the wind or sun. Placing it in the shade and against a protective wall or fence is always a wise measure.

■ Rabbits can be kept in indoor hutches, but in that case it is best to provide regular access to a grassy run.

Note: incidentally, hares and rabbits don't like living together. And guess who usually wins in a scrap between hare and rabbit? Surprisingly, it's the rabbit.

■ Exercise runs

Either make a permanent run, at least 100 x 200 cm/40 x 80 in, with wire-mesh sides which must be sunk into the ground at their base or,

Important

Runs and hutches must be cleaned out two or three times weekly as rabbits urinate abundantly.

Wood logs

A small deciduous wood log should be placed in the wire-fronted 'living room' for gnawing – good for the teeth and saves wear on the hutch itself.

better, build a portable tent-shaped run of mesh with a rigid wooden 'skirting-board' and wire mesh floor which is frequently moved around. The latter avoids the problem of the ground within the run becoming 'sick' and overloaded with germs or parasites. Exercise runs must be covered at one end to afford shelter from sun and rain. Burrowing out is seldom any problem.

Although some rabbits do not object to a harness and lead, not many agree to go 'walkies' like this handsome English rabbit.

Guinea pigs

Guinea pigs are less hardy than rabbits and demand more protection from the elements. Nevertheless, they tolerate a wide range of temperatures provided that there are no draughts and they are protected from damp. If they have plenty of warm bedding in which they can burrow, they can be kept without any form of heating although it is best not to use outdoor hutches during the winter months. For breeding a temperature between 15.5-18.5°C/59-66°F is recommended. If the temperature is not kept above 13°C/55°F, young guinea pigs do not thrive well. Conversely, if the temperature rises above 32°C/90°F heat exhaustion, particularly in pregnant females, may occur and this can be fatal. In very hot weather, provide the animals and their accommodation with some shade.

■ Housing a guinea pig
■ Hutches
Quarters for a guinea pig can be a hutch (as for a rabbit), which should be at least 120 x 60 x 45 cm/48 x 24 x 18 in to house two small guinea pigs.

■ Cages

A cage similar to that used for a hamster but larger, is also suitable for guinea pigs.

■ Pens

You can also house guinea pigs in a pen (loose-box) in a suitable shed or room.

Note: whatever housing is provided, it must be well insulated, well lit, vermin-proof and with sound, water-proof, draught-proof walls

Guinea pigs require a spacious hutch with plenty of clean bedding, e.g. hay, wood shavings or peat moss litter.

Long-haired guinea pigs will require regular grooming.

and flooring. Cages with wire floors are sometimes used for guinea pigs but can lead to trouble with broken legs. The risk can be minimized by using wire with a 1.25 x 3.5 cm/^{1}/$_2$ x 1^1/$_2$ in rectangular mesh.

■ Bedding

This may be wood shavings, preferably from seasoned softwood, or peat moss litter. It is best not to use straw or shavings from green or pine wood which may be eaten and give rise to tummy upsets. Some of the hay provided ad lib will be used by the animals as bedding. Bedding should be removed and the guinea pig quarters cleaned out at least once a week.

Outdoor runs

As with rabbits, outdoor runs (permanent or portable) should be set up for use in good weather. Although a rabbit and a guinea pig will often live happily together particularly if introduced to one another when young, I don't recommend it. There is a tendency for the heavier rabbit to jump on and squash the poor cavy.

Hamsters

In the wild, hamsters live in desert areas with extremes of temperature that can range from 52°C to -3°C/128°F to 25°F within the space of twenty-four hours. They are hermits who prefer to live alone, accustomed to burrows where the atmosphere is one of high humidity.

■ Housing a hamster

As pets, hamsters are best kept singly for most of the time. You can buy special hamster cages at least 2400 cm² x 30 cm high, which should be made of fibre-glass, heavy-duty plastic (polypropylene and polycarbonate are tougher and more hamster-resistant than polyethylene, acrylene and polystyrene), or galvanized metal but not aluminium, zinc or wood which are all easily chewed through by these animals.

Breeding hamsters requires careful planning; turn to page 89 for more detailed information.

This is a typical design for a hamster cage.

■ Hamsters and other rodents love hiding away in corners so if you buy a circular cage, be sure to provide a hidey-hole area.

■ A metal grille at the top or side is preferable to a wire mesh. Hamsters should not be kept in cages where there is wire mesh with fewer than eight meshes per 5 cm/2 in as too big a mesh can cause facial or leg injuries.

■ Slide doors are preferable to hinged ones that easily trap tiny limbs.

■ As with rabbits, access from the side is preferable to access from above the animal.

■ Temperature range

The best temperature range for the hamster environment is 21-24°C/ 70-76°F. Keep pregnant and nursing females and their young at the top end of this range and males towards the bottom. Too high a temperature is more dangerous to hamsters than one that is too low, and high temperatures and low humidity can lead to a shortened life and premature old age. In hot weather, make sure that your hamster cage is in a room where the window is open. Don't stand cages by sunlit windows.

■ Humidity

Ideally, humidity in the hamster cage should not fall below forty to sixty per cent. To this end, make sure that water bottles are always full and stand a bowl of water near the hamster cage in dry weather.

■ Exercising wheels

These are best included in the hamster cage as fixed units which are unable to topple over.

■ Bedding

This must be provided in the form of softwood sawdust or shavings, shredded paper (not newspaper – the ink can be poisonous), woodwool, hay or straw on top of, ideally, a base layer of peat. Try to obtain clean bedding which is uncontaminated by wild rodent droppings or urine. Hamsters like cotton wool as a nest-making material. You should clean out soiled bedding every two or three days. The provision of a small glass jar which is laid on its side in the cage often stimulates the hamster to use it as a lavatory. Empty the jar and wash it out daily.

Exercise wheels and hidey-holes will keep your hamster amused.

Gerbils, mice and rats

Gerbils, rats and mice are easy and cheap to house, and cages of wood, aluminium, galvanized iron or heavy plastic, or aquarium tanks of glass may be used. Wood has the disadvantage of absorbing liquid and is therefore less hygienic. It is also highly chewable!

Cages do allow the inhabitants more opportunities to climb and smell their owners as well as see them, but can be draughty. Glass tanks are cosy, draught-free and easier to clean but require more frequent cleaning because of condensation and tend to be a bit smellier. As each species has its own special requirements, I shall deal with their housing needs separately, but for all, square or rectangular cages or tanks are preferable to circular ones. Rodents adore corners!

Gerbils

■ A heavy plastic or steel and wire cage or an aquarium tank with an area of at least 1500 cm² and 30 cm high with a close-fitting wire mesh lid are ideal.

This cage is ideal for gerbils who like climbing.

■ The floor covering should be of peat moss, potting compost or softwood shavings, with hay, woodwool or shredded paper (not newsprint) for bedding.

■ Artificial fibre bedding should not be used – the strands can get wrapped around tiny limbs, sometimes causing serious interference with blood circulation. Sand, likewise, is not recommended. Gerbils will burrow in it and may easily injure their faces.

■ The room temperature for gerbils should be 15-20°C/59-68°F with a maximum of fifty per cent humidity.

Mice

■ Metal cages or glass tanks are best for mice – minimum dimensions are 1200 cm² x 30 cm high. Each mouse must have at least 260 cm² of floor space.

■ The cage bottom should be solid and the lid tight-fitting.

■ A sleeping compartment may be provided but is not essential if there is plenty of bedding.

Rats love company – don't keep one on its own.

■ The floor covering should be peat moss, softwood, sawdust, wood shavings or chips, with shredded paper (not newsprint) or cotton wool as bedding. Plenty of nesting material cuts down the risk of fighting when strangers (particularly males) are introduced.

■ Ideally, the temperature should be between 15-27°C/59-81°F. Anything above 30°C/88°F can result in fatal heatstroke.

■ When planning housing for mice, bear in mind the probability of future breeding, and either be ready to provide a second cage or tank or ensure that the original one is big enough for an expanding family. Very roughly, an increase of fifty per cent in floor area allows you to house double the number of animals.

Rats

■ Pet shop cages for rats are frequently too small. Rats love company so it is best to keep a pair or a small group. They prefer long narrow cages with plenty of height, a selection of platforms at various levels on which to nest and a toilet area away from food and bedding. Two rats can be housed in a cage with a floor area of 2000 cm² and a minimum height of 30 cm.

■ The floor must be solid. Grille or mesh floors hurt rats' feet.

■ A rabbit hutch, parrot cage or large aquarium tank can be modified to accommodate rats happily. Hutches are more fun for rats than glass tanks.

■ The housing should be lined with peat moss, softwood shavings or sawdust, and shredded paper (not newsprint) should be provided

This cage would be better if it was longer and higher.

for bedding. Cotton wool is not desirable as strands can become entangled with rats' limbs.

■ Rats should be housed indoors in temperatures ideally between 15-27°C/59-82°F. As with the other small rodents, too high a temperature (above 30°C/88°F) can induce heat stroke.

■ Your pets should be given a lump or log of deciduous wood on which to exercise their front teeth.

Furnishing your pet's house

■ Food and water utensils

It is important that you buy the right sort of food and water containers for your pets. Food pots must be gnaw-resistant and heavy enough not to be easily knocked over. Avoid plastic ones – apart from the tendency of both rabbits and rodents to chew them, some

Water bottles like this are better than bowls.

Drinking bowls

■ Shallow bowls and pots, of whatever material, are not good as water containers. They quickly become contaminated with bedding, droppings and food.

individuals are allergic to the colouring pigments in the plastic. Glazed earthenware and stainless steel dishes or bowls are best.

■ In a rabbit hutch, food hay should be placed in a hayrack attached to one of the solid walls in the living room. This avoids trampling and soiling of the hay.

■ Use the gravity-feed demand-type water bottle preferably, but not always, with a ball-valve in its metal spout and which clips on to the cage side or the roof grille. Various designs are available at pet shops. When installing the water bottle make sure that any baby animals can reach the spout and are strong enough to activate the valve.

■ Food and water utensils must be cleaned two or three times a week.

■ Leisure and comfort

Small rodents love the privacy of a nesting box within their house. You can buy these from pet shops in a wide range of designs but the animals will be just as happy with a washed and dried empty milk carton or similar container. Cardboard tubes (from used toilet rolls) are great for mice and gerbils.

■ Exercise and fun accessories

■ Rabbits need exercise and the provision of a run or periods of freedom in a garden are very important. A ramp leading from one of the hutch doors to the ground, which can be put in place during

A wide variety of accessories
can be found in pet shops.

the day to allow the animal free access and entry, is desirable
wherever possible.

■   I mentioned gnawing logs or blocks for rabbits and rats earlier,
but all the small rodents benefit by having some chunk, twig or
branch of softwood to nibble.

■   The small rodent pets, particularly the rats, like to climb. Shelves,
ramps, ladders and climbing devices give them abundant interest,
exercise and entertainment. If they are made of wood, thorough

Devices such
as these
entertain your
pets and
provide
hideaways.

Cardboard tubes are just as effective and as much fun as more expensive accessories and toys.

and regular cleaning of these accessories is essential. Metal is always to be preferred to wood.

■ This also applies to 'treadmill' wheels. Plastic ones don't last like metal types. For stability it is best to have the wheels fixed to some part of the housing. By the way, 'treadmills' are not cruel. The animals love them and can go on and off when they wish.

■ Hamsters are especially fond of wheels as are young rats and mice. Don't, however, supply your gerbils with a wheel. They sometimes damage their tails on them. What is OK for gerbils is a dish or a small 'sand-box' filled with Fuller's earth or some washed fine sand – bought from a pet shop or hardware store, but not dug up outdoors – in which they can give themselves 'dust baths'.

■ You will find all sorts of toys – bells, mirrors, balls etc. – for gerbils at a pet shop, and the ones made for budgerigars please gerbils equally.

CHAPTER FOUR

Food for the small pet

Rabbits

Wild rabbits will eat almost anything, as the horticulturalist and arable farmer know only too well. They munch the poisonous foxglove and deadly nightshade (dangerous for pet rabbits) without any ill effects, but tend to leave the less poisonous ragwort alone. They don't like azalea, rhododendron, honeysuckle, hawthorn, dogwood, sorrel, comfrey (enjoyed by many a pet rabbit), burdock, cowslip or primrose and will usually eat nettles only under the pressure of food shortages. However, some people successfully make nettle silage for pet

Daily requirements

■ A medium-sized rabbit will need about 170 g (6 oz) of greens daily.

■ Pregnant does are fed as above but the amounts must be increased gradually to twice the normal feed by the end of pregnancy.

■ Lactating does need more again. Increase the amount to three times the normal feed by the end of lactation (six to eight weeks after giving birth).

rabbits, by cutting fresh young nettles and pressing them down in a small pit or suitable framework during the summer months. When the silage container is full, a layer of earth is spread on top. The resultant silage cuts nicely during winter, is very nutritious and makes most rabbits' mouths water at suppertime.

Curiously, rabbits seem to detest the cuckoo pint, or arum, and yet this plant is also called pain de lievre, or hare's bread, supposedly a staple ingredient of the hare's diet.

■ Pet rabbit food

There are several different feeding regimes for domestic rabbits. These include the following:

■ Complete foods

One commonly used method is to feed them on one of the 'complete', specially compounded rabbit foods available commercially. They usually come in the form of pellets and some contain a harmless chemical to prevent the onset of a common rabbit disease called coccidiosis (see page 105). These pellets are built up from foods such as oats, bran, grass meal and white fish meal. An average adult rabbit

Note: it is best to wash all green vegetables as well, to avoid the risk of pesticides which may be lingering on their leaves.

will need around 150 g (5 oz) of such pellets daily. Theoretically, no other food needs to be provided, apart of course from fresh water ad lib, but there are good reasons for not sticking to such a strict scientific approach, and reducing the amount of pellets to around 50 g (1³/₄ oz) a day and supplementing them with other foods.

■ Hay and vegetables

I strongly advise the provision of hay, which stops rabbits developing bad habits, such as hair chewing. You must also consider the boredom factor. Rabbits, like humans, don't simply take on food as fuel; there's a delight in variety, in freshness, in the multitude of smells and tastes that make food preparation an art form. Certainly use the rabbit pellets as the core of the diet, but green foods and

Providing a range of appetizing, nutritious food for your rabbit or rodent is important.

'Complete' rabbit food

Rabbit munch

Rabbit munch

Premixed rodent food

Water

roots, such as Brussels sprouts, cabbage, carrots, cauliflower, celery, chicory, kale, parsnip, pears, peas, pea pods, spinach, swede and turnip, should be added as they come into season.

■ Pick wild plants, such as dandelion leaves, clover, coltsfoot, comfrey, cow parsnip, knapweed, shepherd's purse and chickweed – but wash them first if they come from hedgerows possibly contaminated by chemical sprays and traffic fumes etc.

⚠ **Note:** never give wilted greens, kitchen or table waste. Forget lettuce for rabbits, despite what the story books say; there's very little nourishment in it and it can give rise to diarrhoea if your pet has too much of it.

■ Water

Although wild rabbits and their domesticated cousins may seldom drink if feeding on succulent plant material with a high water content, clean, fresh water must always be at hand for pet rabbits – winter and summer. Make sure the water bottles don't freeze in winter. You can always wrap them in an old sock.

Mixing rabbit food concentrates

Some owners prefer to mix up their own rabbit food concentrate instead of using pellets. Grain and other ingredients can be bought from agricultural merchants.

■ Recipes for three such mixes are as follows:
1 Four parts wholemeal bread, one part bran.
2 Equal parts oats, wheat and linseed meal.
3 Four parts oats, four parts barley and two parts soya bean meal.

Note: these 'mashes' can be fed dry or crumbled into warm water or milk.

Poisonous plants

Wild plants which you must never feed to domestic rabbits include: anemone, wild arum, autumn crocus, bindweed, bluebells, bryony, buttercup, celandine, dog mercury, elder, figwort, fool's parsley, foxglove, hemlock, henbane, nightshades, poppy, toadflax and traveller's joy or wild clematis.

■ Daily requirements

A rabbit eats approximately four per cent of its body weight in food each day, so an adult rabbit of, say, 4.5 kg (10 lb) in weight would need around 75 g (2^1/$_2$ oz) of such a concentrate mixture daily, plus about 100 g (3^1/$_2$ oz) of good hay. Although hay is best provided ad lib, it is unwise to give unlimited quantities of concentrates. Rabbits easily lay down wads of excess fat and it can drastically shorten their lives.

■ Diet and tooth disease

Recently some experts have suggested that because of the high incidence of tooth disease in pet rabbits, which can have extremely serious consequences, it would be best to omit concentrates from the diet altogether and feed the animals in a manner more closely resembling that of their wild relations where the teeth and jaws are constantly well exercised. They recommend nothing but ad lib hay and good fresh greens.

■ Freshness

If you have only one or two rabbits, don't buy large quantities of foodstuffs. It is better to buy small quantities of fresh materials frequently. Stored pellets and other forms of concentrates lose valuable vitamins, essential oils etc.

■ Vitamins and minerals

A block of mineral lick should always be hung in the rabbit's quarters. Instinctively your pet will lick and nibble this to obtain any extra minerals he needs. It is also a wise precaution to supplement the water supply with vitamin drops. Suitable preparations are available at the pet shop – follow the dosage directions on the label.

A mineral lick block will enable your rabbit to take instinctively as many minerals as it requires.

Summary for feeding rabbits

The basic rules for feeding rabbits are:
- ■ Weigh concentrates
- ■ Supply moderate and varied quantities of greens and roots in season
- ■ Never neglect water
- ■ Make sure your pet gets lots of exercise

Guinea pigs

Guinea pigs are, of course, vegetarians and resemble other rodents in many respects but they do have some special requirements. Take, for example, vitamin C. Most other animals make this vitamin within their bodies, but the guinea pig – along with man, the great apes, the fruit bat and (as if you haven't guessed) the red-vented bulbul bird – must get adequate vitamin C from its food to avoid going down with scurvy. Other essential elements in the guinea pig's diet are vitamins E and K and an unidentified factor which is present in hay. Hay must be given to stop animals eating their bedding or 'barbering' (chewing each other's hair).

■ The correct diet

A correct diet for guinea pigs is composed of concentrates (in mash or pellet form), which are obtainable from pet shops, together with green food, hay and water. In green food I include fruit and certain root crops.

- ■ Change the different ingredients on successive days to give as much variety as possible.
- ■ Wash all greens and thaw out any frozen roots before feeding.
- ■ Offer only fresh food, removing any spoiled portions.

■ Make sure the hay is free of thistles which can damage those delicate little mouths.

■ Daily feeding requirements

If you give about a tablespoon of some of the items in each of the following groups to your guinea pig every day, you can be sure that all the ingredients essential for a healthy life are included:

1 Dandelion, groundsel, shepherd's purse, cow parsley, sow thistle, cover, chickweed, plantains, vetches, varieties of grass.

2 Carrot, turnip, cabbage, lettuce, kale, marigolds, bramble cuttings, prunings from elm and ash.

3 Boiled potatoes, bread, oats and dog biscuits.

4 Fruit: apples, bananas, grapes, peaches and pears.

5 Cow or sheep pellets, proprietary rodent or guinea-pig foods from the pet shop.

6 Hay – this should always be fed ad lib.

■ Water

Adequate, clean, fresh water must always be available. Even when your pet is taking in lots of green foods, you cannot rely on him getting all the water he needs that way. Too dry a diet can lead to prolapse of the rectum. Although commercial guinea-pig pellets are supplemented with vitamin C, it is best to dissolve a 250 mg tablet of vitamin C into the animal's water every time you change it, which should be at least three times a week.

Note: once a week it is a good idea to give a pinch of bone meal (sterilized) and a pinch of dried yeast. In the winter, a drop of cod liver oil should be mixed with the food every two or three days.

Hamsters

Hamsters are easy to feed and there are several ways of going about it. Variety is essential, and you can try feeding grains, carrots, clover (but not grass), dandelions, salad, bread, fruit, scraps of fish and meat, dog biscuits (good for the teeth) and milk. Pelleted or other forms of ready-prepared food for rodents, mice, laboratory animals or dogs can be obtained from pet shops and provide an excellent balanced core to the diet. A pinch of brewer's yeast, or half a yeast tablet, once or twice a week is recommended, particularly to prevent 'wet tail' (see page 119).

■ Feeding guidelines

■ Hamsters can be given ad lib quantities of food but do be sure to clean out uneaten portions daily, otherwise your pets will hoard them and they will decay.

■ Do not store foods for long periods (they lose their vitamin content) and make sure they do not become contaminated with wild rodent droppings.

■ Wash all fruit and green food before feeding.

■ It is normal for hamsters to eat their own droppings. The latter contain vitamins B and K which are produced in the bowels.

■ Water

A supply of fresh clean water must always be available. Never let a water bottle run dry. Lack of water for twenty-four hours can cause a weight loss of 10 g ($^1/_3$ oz) or more; in youngsters, particularly in warm weather, it may have fatal results.

Note: some hamsters adore bits of bread and butter sandwich. Take it easy! Too much fat can cause 'wet tail', heart trouble and convulsions. Similarly, trim any fat off scraps of meat that are fed to your pet.

Gerbils

Some desert-dwelling species
of gerbil survive on wind-
blown seeds and little else.
Most gerbils prefer to take
food back to their
burrows to eat and those
that inhabit the colder
regions are hamster-like
in their hoarding.
Mongolian gerbils have
been known to store as much
as 20 kg (44 lb) of seeds.

■ A balanced diet

As pets, gerbils need a basic balanced diet with a fairly high
protein content supplemented with a variety of other items to keep

Home-made gerbil mix

Typically, gerbil/hamster mixes contain seeds, grains, nuts,
dried vegetables and some dried egg. If you want to make your
own gerbil mix, take equal parts of the following:
■ Seeds (sunflower, linseed etc.)
■ Oats, wheat, flaked maize, wheat germ, millet,
   sugarless cereals
■ Peanuts
■ Store the mixture in a well-sealed tin in a cool, dry place.

Note: one mature gerbil will eat about one tablespoonful of
the mix per day.

them interested. Premixed diets, which are suitable for both hamsters and gerbils, are available at pet shops as are balanced pellet foods for rabbits, mice and rats, which are also suitable. Check on the packet label to see that the protein content is at least twenty per cent and that the food is not past its sell-by date.

■ Vegetables and fruit

Other foods which can be given occasionally include the following: vegetables, washed and dried greens and roots, washed and dried wild plants, such as dandelion, chickweed and clover, and fruit of all kinds. Remember that only thorough washing removes all traces of pesticides, so wash all fresh fruit, vegetables and plants before feeding them to your pet.

⚠ Caution

Sunflower seeds are very rich in fat and low in calcium. Gerbils adore them, and if they eat too many, obesity and skeletal disease can result. Too much in the way of green vegetables, particularly items like lettuce with a high water content, can cause digestive upsets and diarrhoea. I repeat that you should give these foods only occasionally and then in small amounts (about one tablespoonful only).

Owners like to treat their gerbil pets to snacks, such as chocolate drops, potato crisps, popcorn etc. These goodies are fine provided they are only given very occasionally. As with us humans, they are terribly fattening for gerbils!

Rats and mice

Wild species eat a whole range of foodstuffs. Brown rats can thrive almost anywhere and will scoff anything from putrid waste and young birds, to rabbit droppings and lubricating grease! More salubriously, the musk rat dines on freshwater mussels and crayfish. A species such as the jumping mouse lives on fruit, seeds and insects and this is typical of the main diet of the majority of the group.

Surprisingly, cheese isn't the thing for your tame mouse or rat. It isn't even one of their favourite foods and too much of it may produce strong-smelling urine.

■ Proprietary foods

Specially balanced proprietary mouse and rat foods can be bought from the pet shop.

■ Best breeding results are obtained with diets containing twenty-five to forty per cent protein.

■ Proprietary foods should be supplemented with a little green food and fruit three times a week.

■ They should not be stored for long, and should be protected from contamination by vermin.

■ Where cereals or food pellets are stored for any length of time, do watch that they don't get infested with mites. Food mites can cause skin disease or digestive upsets in your pets.

■ Home-made mixes

■ **For mice** If you want to make up your own diets, a good one for mice is four parts oats, one part canary seed and one part white millet. In addition, give a little dandelion, chickweed, apple or raw

dark green vegetable on alternate days. Kitchen scraps can be used in small quantities but do remember to clean out old food every day.

■ **For rats** You can use a variable mixture of some of the following: dog biscuit, bran, oats, beans, cabbage, carrots, bread, fruit, bits of cooked meat or fish, milk, hard-boiled egg. Meat and fish are best given only once or twice weekly. A drop of cod liver oil and a tiny pinch of dried yeast once a week are also valuable supplements. Both mice and rats can be fed ad lib, but again, you must clean out all remains of food every day.

Water

For rats and mice, fresh, clean water must be available at all times, even though they may drink little.

CHAPTER FIVE

Breeding

Rabbits

You'll find that it's no joke about the rabbit's enthusiasm for multiplication; suffice it to say that after being introduced into Australia, rabbits took a mere fifty years to colonize that vast island.

Rabbits don't have an oestrus – heat-cycle – (unlike rodents) and can breed at any time of year. Ovulation, the shedding of ripe eggs from the ovary, does not occur spontaneously as in women or in animals such as the bitch or cow, but is triggered by the act of mating. January to June is the main breeding season with wild rabbits having a particular fancy for March and April.

■ Litters

Rabbits can have several litters of two to eight young each year. The average litter size is five but it can be as large as ten. The most prolific breed of rabbit is the Norfolk Star, which can produce ninety to a hundred young per year; one famous Norfolk Star buck named 'Chewer' fathered over 40,000 offspring between 1968 and 1973! The general rule, though, should be not to exceed three litters per year for the sake of the health and long life of your pet doe.

■ Mating

If there is no oestrus cycle in rabbits, how do you know when to put the buck and the doe together? Oestrus, the time when ripe eggs are present in the ovary, can sometimes be detected by observing the vulva which may enlarge and become purplish at this time. However, this sign isn't always present and, even if it is, some does won't accept the buck. The test is to see how the doe reacts when introduced to the buck – always take the doe to the buck, never the reverse, otherwise the male may be too busy investigating his strange surroundings to concentrate on things amorous. If you have more

Nest building

The babies are usually prepared for by the doe who makes a nest lined with soft fur plucked from her own coat. It is best to provide a shallow nest-box, 5-7 cm (2-3 in) deep, in the sleeping compartment of the hutch. The box is lined with sawdust and hay or straw chopped into lengths of 10-15 cm (4-6 in). If the doe does not contribute much fur to the nest on the day before she gives birth, add some tufts of fur saved from previous pregnancies if possible.

than one buck, try the doc with each of them. Sometimes the lady shows her fickle nature by turning down one suitor only to fling herself passionately at the next.

■ Pregnancy

Pregnancy lasts around one month (twenty-eight to thirty-four days) in rabbits but approximately forty-seven days in hares. Does may accept the buck at any time during pregnancy or false pregnancy.

■ **False pregnancy** (pseudo-pregnancy) is a common phenomenon in rabbits and can last about two-and-a-half weeks. The milk glands swell and the doe may actually begin to prepare a nest for her phantom young. False pregnancy can be due to an infertile mating, although it frequently follows a successful mating where the embryos die and are resorbed into the mother's body some time during the pregnancy period. It is reckoned that more than half the litters actually conceived are resorbed in this way. This curious 'change of mind' by the doe's body is perfectly normal in most cases and seems to be Nature's last-minute attempt at population control. An expert can detect pregnancy by gently feeling the doe's abdomen as early as nine days after mating.

■ Birth

The young are generally born at night. The event is rarely observed by the owner, the whole process taking ten to thirty minutes with seldom any complications demanding veterinary assistance. Very occasionally there is a gap of several hours or even a day between the birth of one part of the litter and another. Each baby is born with its placenta (afterbirth) which the doe eats – a sensible provision by Nature that prevents fouling of the nest. After being licked clean by their mother, the babies (sometimes called kittens) promptly seek out the maternal teats and start suckling. If necessary, kittens can be fostered onto another doe if the latter's young are the same age and the switch is begun before they are three weeks old.

■ In normal births to does having a first litter, about one per cent of babies are stillborn. Overall, the ratio of male to female babies is exactly 50:50.

■ If a doe is mated while suckling a small litter she can become

These very young kittens are wild European rabbits.

True or false?

Up to the middle of the eighteenth century there were occasional reports, sometimes emanating from learned medical sources, of women giving birth to rabbits. In 1726, Mary Toft of Godalming in Surrey, England, achieved considerable notoriety by her extensively circulated statements that she bore rabbits. Mr St. André, surgeon and anatomist to the Royal Household, published a pamphlet supporting her story with engravings of the rabbits 'taken from life'. Other eminent doctors also backed her up. Eventually, after being closely watched, the curious Ms Toft was exposed and confessed to being a fraud, but for a short time thereafter rabbit was excluded from most English dining-tables.

pregnant, whereas if she is suckling a larger litter (the minimum size varies with breed) the pregnancy will be curtailed after about five days.

■ Gradually increase the food of a pregnant doe so that at the time of birth she should be getting three times the normal ration. It is a good idea to put a shelf into a breeding hutch so that the mother can get some respite from time to time from the incessant demands of her brood.

■ Development of the kittens

At birth young rabbits are helpless, with their eyes and ears closed and only a light down instead of fur. By the end of the first week of life the fur begins to grow; after ten days the eyes open; after twelve days the ears open; and by sixteen to eighteen days the kittens have begun to leave the nest and to nibble solid food.

■ **Note:** do not touch the kittens before they begin to emerge from the nest. If you do, the doe may kill them. Does may also kill their

young if they have too little milk and sometimes for psychological
reasons that are not understood.

■ Feeding the kittens

■ The kittens suckle for six to eight weeks and after weaning should
be kept in pairs or colonies, although young males are best housed
singly from three months of age to prevent fighting. It is possible to
raise a baby rabbit on the bottle, but cow's milk isn't rich enough for
the job since it contains only four per cent protein, whereas rabbit
milk contains ten per cent.

■ **Making formula milk** To make a suitable formula, extra protein in
the form of 15 g ($^1/_2$ oz) of calcium caseinate per 280 g (10 fl oz) of
cow's milk must be added. This mixture is suitable until the kittens are
seven days old after which the calcium caseinate must be increased to
17 g per 280 g of milk. At fourteen days, the caseinate must be raised
yet again to 20 g per 280 g of milk. The caseinate is mixed with the
milk by whisking in a blender and will keep for several days in a
refrigerator. Feeds should be given every three hours, beginning at
6 am and finishing at midnight. The milk mixture should be warmed
to blood heat before feeding and presented to the infant by pipette
or, best of all, from a doll's feeding bottle complete with teat.

Reproductive life

Rabbits become sexually mature at four months (small breeds)
or six months (large breeds). Don't breed for the first time until
young does are at least six months old (small breeds) or ten
months old (large breeds). Males have an active reproductive
life of three to four years. Females should be retired from
breeding at two to three years of age. The life span of rabbits is
six or seven years on average, although the record is held by a
doe that reached eighteen years!

Guinea pigs

Female guinea pigs become sexually mature as early as four to five weeks of age. Males are fertile somewhat later at eight to ten weeks. If breeding is your aim, a good age to start mating a female is when she is twelve to thirteen weeks old, while the bones of her birth canal are still flexible and are able to 'give' easily during birth.

■ Mating

The female guinea pig, usually called appropriately the 'sow', can be allowed to mix freely with the male or 'boar' while she is not pregnant. You can keep one sow and one boar or as many as twelve sows and one boar in a breeding group. Unlike hamsters, there are no special mating instructions for the peaceable guinea pig.

A nest box with around 0.25 m^2 (2.6 sq ft) of floor area, lined with soft hay or shredded paper (not newsprint), can be laid on for a pregnant sow, but is not essential provided you make sure there is plenty of bedding hay available to her in which she can form a nest for herself.

These sociable creatures get on well in groups and even after the birth it is perfectly correct, if there is adequate space, to leave a bunch of mums and their broods together for communal rearing. It is best, however, to remove the boar, or boars, from the sows if you suspect that the latter are pregnant or at least as soon as the young are born. Some owners leave a boar and several sows permanently

together and such gradually enlarging colonies are rarely the scene of disharmony or squabbling, but the steady population expansion will certainly lead to epidemics of disease if enough living space is not provided. In these communal systems each sow needs a minimum of approximately 1300 cm^2 (200 in^2) of floor space. Some experts consider that the optimum colony size is one boar to twelve sows.

■ Courtship displays

During mating, you may witness the courtship display typical of guinea pigs (and also of certain other rodents such as chinchillas, agoutis, coypus and porcupines). The male wags his rear end, quivers his body and makes sprightly hops. He also sprays urine on his mate.

■ Oestrus

The female has an oestrus cycle of five to six days and is 'in heat' for only a few hours. Once mated, the female rapidly becomes non-receptive to the male. Oestrus commonly occurs soon after the birth of a litter and there is no harm in mating a female again at this time.

Pregnancy

In the guinea pig, this lasts from fifty-nine to seventy-two days with an average of sixty-three days. Litter size is between one and thirteen with an average of four. Two or three litters are born each year under suitable conditions and the mother suckles her young for two to three months. Wild cavies produce young only once a year with only one or two babies to a litter but these little fellows begin feeding themselves at one day old.

Hamsters

Female hamsters normally become mature at the early age of six to eight weeks although successful mating has been recorded in animals only four weeks old. If you want to breed hamsters, use young females, preferably ones under eight months of age. A good time is when they are about two months old. The duration of pregnancy is the shortest for any mammal that produces fully developed babies: fifteen to eighteen days. Several litters can be produced in a year, each averaging four to twelve young.

■ Mating

The oestrus (heat) cycle lasts about four days. To test whether a female is on heat, place her in a container, such as a large tin lined with paper, or even a bucket, and introduce a male. If she is on heat she will flatten her spine and then arch it downwards and accept the male. Keep an eye on things in case fighting breaks out. If the couple get on well, leave them together for fifteen minutes to one hour, but

Baby hamsters suckle from their mother for a period of three to four weeks before taking solids.

still remain alert for trouble. If there is no sign of spine-flattening within ten minutes of the introduction, return the female to her cage and repeat the procedure on the following day.

■ **False pregnancy** (pseudo-pregnancy) sometimes occurs and can last for eight to ten days.

■ Pregnancy

The female hamster's cage should be placed in a quiet place when she is pregnant. Darken the part of the cage over the nest by covering it with a suitable piece of metal or plastic. Shredded paper, in strips not more than about 0.5 cm ($^1/_4$ in) wide, is the best material for bedding in a breeding cage. It is clean and won't entangle the new-born babies.

■ Birth

This is usually a trouble-free process that occurs at night. The mother will suckle her young for three to four weeks. Make sure that she has all the food she wants during the pregnancy and lactation period.

Gerbils

In the wild, gerbils organise themselves into large social groups comprising between one and three adult males, two to seven adult females and several subadults and juveniles. They all live together in a jealously guarded burrow, chasing off strange gerbils should any come a-calling – with one exception, which prevents the gerbils becoming dangerously inbred. Female gerbils leave their group when they come into oestrus (heat), visit another burrow where they are permitted to enter, get mated, and then return to their own community. The young born thereafter are brought up not by their mother and father, but by their mother and 'uncles'.

This female gerbil is carrying a baby into her nesting box.

■ Mating

Pet gerbils can breed at any time of the year although most sexual activity is in the summer. If you decide to pair a couple of gerbils, it is best to do this before they are sexually mature, at nine to ten weeks old, and to use a pair from the same litter. Unrelated gerbils, particularly adults, can fight furiously – even to the death – and introducing such individuals requires much care, supervision and patience by the owner who should at first arrange brief encounters which, little by little, can be extended as the days go by.

■ Oestrus and pregnancy

Female gerbils come into oestrus (heat) every four to ten days until they are fifteen to twenty months old. During her breeding life one female may produce up to ten litters (one litter every thirty to forty days) with an average litter size of five pups. If a female is mated at the first oestrus after giving birth while still suckling more than two pups, the resulting pregnancy may be extended by means of the natural physiological mechanism called delayed implantation. Such a long pregnancy can last for up to forty-two days. Normally pregnancy lasts for twenty-four to twenty-six days.

■ If a non-fertile mating occurs, it is occasionally followed by a false pregnancy of fourteen to sixteen days.

■ Diet during pregnancy

When a female is pregnant (you may suspect this having watched the mating or heard the rhythmic drumming of the male gerbil's hind legs as he becomes sexually excited), cut down on fattening food like sunflower seeds but increase the amount of protein in the diet by adding a little dried milk powder to the food.

■ Birth

A nest-box is not essential for an expectant gerbil mum, but extra supplies of bedding in the form of soft paper should be provided for her to use in nest construction. It isn't necessary to remove the male when birth occurs. Gerbils are monogamous and the male will generally do no harm to growing pups.

■ Around seventy-five per cent of newborn pups survive – weak ones are born dead or die during the first few days after birth. Don't be too upset – it is natural, and almost all of the pups that perish are congenitally defective in some way.

■ Sometimes mothers will kill and eat their litters or desert them.

This can be caused by the stress of excessive disturbance, overcrowding or the presence of disease in the mother's breast tissue. Less frequently, males exhibit cannibalism (jealousy perhaps?) but usually they make good fathers.

■ Baby gerbils are born hairless, deaf, blind and toothless but grow amazingly quickly and for that reason the mother's food should be increased immediately after giving birth. Hair starts to grow at six days old and eyes open at ten to twelve days.

■ The pups begin eating solids at between sixteen and twenty days and are weaned at twenty-one to twenty-four days.

■ After weaning the youngsters can remain in the parental cage, but they should be sexed at eight weeks and males and females then placed in separate new accommodation – otherwise inbreeding is likely to begin.

Two-week-old gerbil babies will soon be ready to begin eating solids.

Mice and rats

■ Mice

Male and female mice can be left together permanently during their breeding life. The heat cycle in the female mouse occurs about every five days. Mice become sexually mature at six to eight weeks. Pregnancy lasts twenty or twenty-one days but can be as long as twenty-eight days where mating occurs at the first heat period after giving birth. Litter size is up to twenty with an average of seven. (A record thirty-two young born to a house mouse in 1961 is the largest litter produced by any wild mammal at a single birth.)

■ Rats

Female rats should be put into separate cages at least one week before giving birth. Rats become sexually mature at between forty and sixty days. The heat cycle lasts four to five days. Pregnancy in

It is very important that baby rodents should not be handled during the first two weeks of life.

Caution

Rats and mice suckle their young for around three weeks. Never handle the young or change the bedding for at least one week after birth, and it is best left until they are two weeks old. At around two weeks of age, mice reach the so-called 'flea age' and, when disturbed, may leap straight up into the air in alarm.

rats lasts twenty-one to twenty-three days. Litter size is up to sixteen with an average of eleven young.

■ Scent and fertility

Odours that contain sex hormones (pheromones) are very important in the sex life of mice. The more female mice that are kept in one enclosure, the more infertile they become; the 'sex smell' of one another reduces their fertility. Male odours work in the opposite way,

but only if the scent comes from the female mouse's own mate. Infidelity, in the form of the introduction of a strange male, not only continues to block the female's fertility but also actually kills any developing embryos within her womb. A puritanical Providence puts the mockers on any hint of mousish permissiveness!

Hand-rearing pet babies

■ Hand-rearing is seldom called for but the necessity could arise if unweaned youngsters were suddenly orphaned for some reason or the mother developed mastitis or agalactia (absence of milk). Of course, in certain circumstances such babies might be fostered by another lactating female with young of approximately the same age.

■ If the mother will not accept the strange baby or babies you can try smearing a touch of menthol vapour rub on both the nose of the foster mother and the bodies of the babies. The menthol masks the 'foreign' scent of the new arrivals.

■ It is often necessary to resort to artificial milk feeding. The sort of milk powder available at pet shops for rearing cats will normally be satisfactory. Make it up with water as for kittens, following the instructions on the packet, and administer by means of an eye-dropper or hypodermic (insulin) syringe obtainable at a pharmacy – without the needle, naturally.

■ Feed a little and often, enough to make the stomach plump, and judge your progress by weighing the babies if you have a small enough scale.

■ Start weaning at the appropriate time (see above) by introducing wholemeal bread soaked in milk or thin oat porridge.

■ Keep the babies warm, preferably by hanging an infra-red bulb (of the type used in bathrooms and by farmers) over them at a distance of no less than 1 m (3 ft) or use a heating pad wrapped in a blanket.

CHAPTER SIX

General care of your pet

■ Hygiene

This is vital in ensuring a long and healthy life for your pet and in controlling unwanted odour.

■ Hutch or cage floor litter should be changed twice a week (daily for does with young).

■ Bedding should be replaced once a week except where unweaned babies are in a nest.

■ The animal's quarters should be carefully cleaned at these times and a mild animal disinfectant spray should be applied and then dried off. Never use phenol/carbolic acid type disinfectants. Buy approved pet disinfectants from the pet shop or use so-called ampholytic disinfectants or the kind used in catering for disinfecting glassware.

■ In summer, rabbit and guinea-pig hutches should be scrubbed thoroughly with hot water and mild disinfectant, rinsed, and then allowed to dry while the occupiers are outside.

Distress in rodents

Do watch out for signs of sudden distress in small rodent pets. Certain noises, including very high pitched ones that cannot be picked up by human ears, can affect these creatures. The source could even be a computer, telephone or television remove control device. If such things are seen to upset your pets, re-site their housing well away from the noise-maker.

Grooming

Rabbits With one exception, do not need grooming; they do it for themselves. However, there is no harm in grooming your rabbit if it gives you and your pet pleasure. Also, it does make the animal tamer and easier to handle as well as assisting the moulting process at the end of the winter. The exception is the luxurious, long-haired Angora. This rabbit must be groomed daily with a soft brush, applying it in the direction of the natural lie of the coat.

Guinea pigs Not essential for most guinea pigs, but some long-haired ones can be groomed using a small, very soft brush.

■ Food and water containers must be cleaned daily, preferably put through a hot wash in a dishwasher or scalded with boiling water.

■ Playtime and grooming

Handle and play with your small pet at least four or five times a week. Feed it tidbits from your fingers and groom it gently with a soft brush. Grooming is desirable but not essential for most of these animals. It is, however, very important for longer haired breeds like the Angora rabbit and Peruvian guinea pig and for any individual whose coat becomes soiled or stained somehow. The grooming equipment made for cats is ideal for rabbits and guinea pigs. Stains and sticky patches can be removed with moist cloths, or you can use the spray made for cleaning birds' feathers, which are available in pet shops.

■ Sexing

It goes without saying that the major requirement, if you decide to breed your small pets is to know what sex they are; not always easy if they are young. Here is how to go about it.

Rabbits

Male rabbits have a round genital opening. Gentle pressure around it will extrude the penis. Female rabbits have a slit-like genital opening.

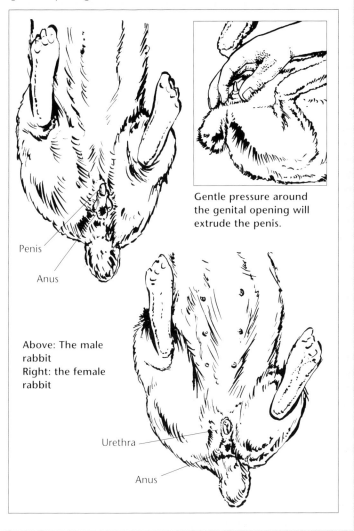

Gentle pressure around the genital opening will extrude the penis.

Penis

Anus

Above: The male rabbit
Right: the female rabbit

Urethra

Anus

Guinea pigs

The genitalia of male and female guinea pigs are very similar at first sight. However, by pressing gently on each side of the genital opening the penis can be extruded in the male.

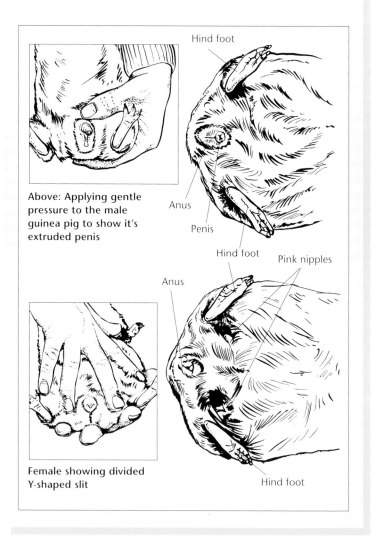

Hind foot

Above: Applying gentle pressure to the male guinea pig to show it's extruded penis

Anus

Penis

Hind foot

Pink nipples

Anus

Female showing divided Y-shaped slit

Hind foot

Hamsters

Even when young, female hamsters are easy to recognise by the lines of teats on their abdomens. When the fur grows you may have to hunt carefully for them. Also, the male has an elongated hind end and there is a prominent bulge just before the tail. The female's hind end is more rounded and has no bulge.

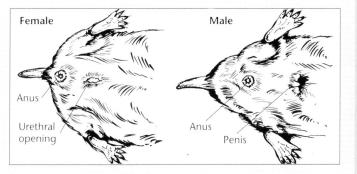

Gerbils

To examine a gerbil's genitalia don't turn it onto its back, but rather (and this is the one occasion when you can do it) raise the animal off the ground by briefly picking it up by the base of its tail. Males have a darkish oblong-shaped scrotum beneath the tail whereas females have a small vagina close to the anus.

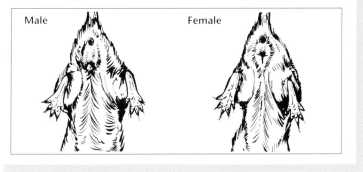

Rats

The distance between the anus and the tiny genital opening is distinctly greater in males than in females (at three weeks of age, for example, 1.25 cm as opposed to just under 1 cm). Also, you should be able to see the slight swelling, even in young males, where the scrotum will be.

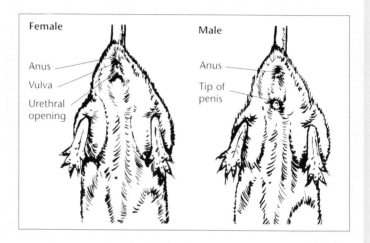

Mice

In mice, as in rats, the distance between the anus and the genital opening is greater (almost twice as far) in males as compared to females. Gentle pressure around the opening will cause the penis to protrude in males.

Sexing is more difficult in very young mice. At two to three weeks of age, females have ten nipples which are clearly visible on their still hairless bellies. At three to four weeks old, gently pulling the skin of the male's rear underbelly towards the front will cause the testes to descend into the scrotum.

CHAPTER SEVEN

When small pets fall ill

Rabbits

Although generally hardy, trouble-free creatures, rabbits do sometimes fall ill and, as a species, have their peculiar problems.

■ Myxomatosis

This is undoubtedly the most notorious rabbit disease. A virus disease, it was first described in 1893 in domestic rabbits in Uruguay. Apparently, the germ is widespread among wild South American rabbits which have built up a comparatively strong resistance to its attack. Attempts to control the rabbit population in Australia were made fairly successfully by introducing the virus, although strains of

✚ The pet-owner's approach to the sick rabbit

As with other sorts of pet, it is essential to seek professional help from a veterinary surgeon if you are troubled by something you do not understand. There are a large number of illnesses that can afflict the different organs and systems of the rabbit. Most have been extensively studied by scientists and treatment methods worked out. As with all medicine, diagnosis is what counts; any fool can read up the treatment if he knows exactly what the matter is.

rabbits resistant to the disease soon appeared.

In 1953, the virus was introduced deliberately into France; quickly it got out of control and swept through the largely non-resistant rabbit population of Europe, causing almost 100 per cent fatalities. It arrived in Britain in October 1953, striking first at colonies in Kent and Sussex. Domestic rabbits, as well as wild ones, can be affected although it does not usually attack hares (except for the Irish blue hare), hamsters, gerbils, mice, rats or guinea pigs.

It is spread by the bite of rabbit fleas in Europe and by mosquitoes in Australia, and also by direct and indirect contact. Among wild rabbits, myxomatosis spreads most rapidly in the spring during their peak breeding season. The reason for this is the intriguing fact that rabbit fleas themselves breed only on pregnant rabbits.

■ Symptoms

After an incubation period of two to eight days, the animal shows signs of a cold with swelling of the nose, ears, eyelids and other body openings. Puffy, jelly-like swellings form beneath the skin over the body. There is dullness, lack of appetite, loss of weight and, finally, death after eleven to eighteen days.

Treatment

This is very difficult, and antibiotics are of little value. Prevention can be achieved by vaccination and controlling fleas or other insect carriers. Domestic rabbits are not commonly at risk nowadays but if you live in the country and have wild rabbits entering your garden, precautions to be taken would include:

■ Proofing the rabbit hutch with wire mesh – five strands per centimetre (ten strands per inch).

■ Using insecticides and restricting the use of runs when you learn of myxomatosis in the area.

■ Best of all is a protective vaccine which is now available. Consult your vet.

Note: gradually, resistant strains of wild rabbit have appeared in Britain although the disease is still very much around.

General symptoms

I have grouped general symptoms of poor health in the following section with some comments on first aid, the vet's approach and a little background.

■ Loss of weight

This can be due to various diseases, including pseudotuberculosis, tapeworm cysts, coccidiosis or other forms of chronic infection. The vet will take specimens of droppings to look for parasitic coccidia or other bugs. If the diagnosis is coccidiosis, drugs such as sulphadimidine, may be prescribed for adding to the drinking water. Where bacteria are the cause, antibiotics are used either by injection or again by medicating the water. Seek advice early.

■ Fur balls

Sometimes loss of weight accompanied by lack of appetite and perhaps diarrhoea is due to fur balls in the stomach. As in long-haired cats, excessive grooming and swallowing of hair gradually builds up a firm, sticky mass within the stomach. Carefully spooning a 5 ml teaspoonful of mineral oil ('liquid paraffin') into the rabbit and gently massaging the abdomen may soften and disperse the fur ball, but, unfortunately, a surgical operation (gastrotomy) under general anaesthetic is usually required.

Consult your vet

Much time, suffering and cash spent on patent medicines can be saved by loading a mopey bunny into a carrying box and whisking him off to the vet's surgery. Many rabbit conditions need the same sort of treatment – antibiotics, injections, simple surgery or whatever – that is given for similar conditions in man, horses, dogs or elephants.

■ Tooth trouble

Wild rabbits seldom visit the dentist. It isn't because they're frightened of the dental chair but because they exercise their teeth cropping grass and other fibre-containing plants and choose a healthy diet. Pet rabbits have too easy a life. Commercial (pet shop) rabbit diets need little chewing, and many owners provide food that is rich in starch and low in roughage. Also, vitamin/mineral deficiencies or imbalances are not unusual. The result is the formation of plaque, caries (cavities), weakening and overgrowth of the teeth. This can then lead on to secondary, potentially serious disease.

■ **Dental problems** are common in rabbits. If you suspect anything is wrong with your rabbit's chewing, if there are any odd lumps about the jaws or if the front teeth seem rather long, consult your vet. Dental check-ups and, where necessary, treatment can ensure a longer life for your pet. Don't try cutting overgrown teeth yourself.

Rabbit's skull

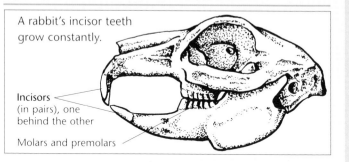

A rabbit's incisor teeth grow constantly.

Incisors (in pairs), one behind the other

Molars and premolars

■ Constipation

If mild and only of one or two days' duration, try adding half a 5 ml teaspoonful of Epsom salts (magnesium sulphate) to the drinking water or buy a 'Micralax' enema from the pharmacist. Use the latter by inserting the nozzle into the rabbit's rectum to a depth of about 1cm ($^1/_2$ in), and then squeeze in approximately one-third of the pre-packed enema.

■ Sometimes you will see a condition known as 'the blows' by rabbit breeders. This is when the large bowel (colon) becomes blocked with hard, dry droppings. Gas forms behind the obstruction, the bloated bowels cause pain and the 'blown-up' rabbit becomes miserable and depressed and may die. The condition occurs most often in half-grown rabbits during the summer months and may be connected with clover feeding. As first aid, you can try the 'Micralax' enema, but seek veterinary help quickly.

■ Diarrhoea

This can be due to bacterial infection, occasionally worms, protozoal parasites (coccidiosis) or other causes. Coccidiosis is the commonest cause and occurs generally where standards of hygiene (overcrowding, inadequate cleaning out etc.) have fallen.

■ **Tyzzer's disease**, caused by a bacterium (Bacillus piliformis), affects rabbits, hamsters, gerbils, rats and mice and is frequently fatal. Diarrhoea and inappetance are symptoms, or, in the chronic form, steady loss of weight and condition. Prompt treatment with tetracycline antibiotics can alleviate but not necessarily eradicate it.

Rabbits with diarrhoea

■ They must be allowed to drink ad lib

■ Do not restrict liquid intake

■ As a first-aid measure, substitute cold camomile tea for the drinking water

■ Keep the patient warm

■ Precise diagnosis usually involves sending samples of droppings to the laboratory

■ Incidentally, should you be unfortunate enough to have your pet die, remember that a post-mortem examination by the veterinary surgeon will give valuable information, particularly where any other animals may be at risk

■ Salmonella infection

Often from rodent-contaminated food or bedding or contact with animals carrying the bacteria (perhaps without symptoms), this does occur sometimes. It can result in death, particularly in young rabbits. Diarrhoea and dullness may be the only symptoms of salmonellosis in pet rabbits.

■ Mucoid enteritis

This is another common cause of diarrhoea. It usually combines diarrhoea with severe emaciation, but is not well understood and may be due to a virus. It affects rabbits of all ages, ending fatally in most unweaned animals and occasionally in adults.

Treatment This depends on correct diagnosis of the kind of diarrhoea. There is no sure treatment for mucoid enteritis. Other forms require anti-parasitic, anti-coccidial or antibiotic drugs.

■ Snuffles

If your pet looks as if it has got a cold or chronic catarrh, it may be the common ailment called 'snuffles'. In its most acute form this disease may show little beyond a nasal discharge, fever and fairly rapid death.

Above: Over-grown rabbit's claws

Above: Correctly trimmed claws

Overgrown claws

If a rabbit's claws become overgrown, the excess nails can be trimmed off. This is best done by a veterinary surgeon, especially in dark-coloured rabbits with dark nails. If you feel competent to trim a pale-coloured rabbit's overgrown claws, use animal nail clippers, which are obtainable from pet shops – they are much better than human-type clippers.

You should be able to see the pink core, or 'quick', of the claw through the translucent 'shell'. This is where the blood vessels and nerves run. Cut at least 1 cm ($^1/_2$ in) in front of the tip of the 'quick'.

Temperature

You may wish to check the temperature of your pet. This can be done by the insertion of a stubby-ended clinical thermometer into the rectum. The normal temperature of a healthy rabbit is between 38.6°C (101.5°F) and 40.1°C (104.2°F) (much higher than in a human) with an average of 39.4°C (103°F). Remember, however, that excitement and handling may produce a rise in temperature.

The mild form exhibits sneezing with no loss of condition. The causes are two bacteria named Pasteurella and Brucella.

Treatment They need treatment from the vet who will use a broad-spectrum antibiotic (one antibiotic, lincomycin, is toxic for rabbits and cannot be used) and may, in chronic cases, prescribe nasal drops. Don't delay in seeking professional help: you may avoid bunny progressing to pneumonia. Keep the patient warm.

■ Skin disease

Apart from some lumps and bumps (see page 111), there are several specific skin complaints of rabbits including rabbit syphilis. This disease is not infectious for humans or other animals and is common in domestic rabbits. It takes the form of weeping sores round the genital area, on the lips, eyelids and nose. Severe ulceration can obstruct the passage of urine and droppings and if the germ spreads to internal organs, the rabbit may die. The bacterium that causes rabbit syphilis is similar to that which causes syphilis in man and it responds to injections of penicillin or other anti-syphilitic drugs.

■ **Ringworm,** mange, various kinds of bacteria and a pox virus infection can also attack the coat of a rabbit. All need diagnosis by the vet, who may take samples for laboratory tests, and there are specific treatments for each kind. Ringworm usually comes from rats and mice, so make sure your hutches and runs are rodent-proof. It can often be treated by drugs added to the rabbit's food.

■ **Loss of hair and 'wet eczema'** of the skin on the under-surface of the hind legs, particularly beneath the 'hocks', or under the belly of the rabbit is often caused by bad flooring (i.e. wire mesh) or lack of sufficient fresh litter on damp, dirty solid floors. Bacteria enter skin abrasions and nasty infections result. Improved housing and management are keys to a cure.

Treatment Antibiotic and antiseptic creams and dressings assist healing.

■ **Ear 'canker'** is the commonest form of mange in the rabbit. Brown or putty-coloured flakes and scabs build up inside the ear and cause the rabbit to scratch the ear with the hind feet.

■ **Prevention** Cleaning the ears regularly (once monthly) with swabs

Fleas

Occasionally rabbits, particularly those kept outdoors and in warm weather, can become infested with fleas. These parasite cause irritation and scratching. Usually there are tell-tale signs of fine black 'coaldust' (actually the dried droppings of fleas) on the skin when the hair is parted.

Treatment is by means of insecticidal sprays or powders of the kind suitable for cats. Because the fleas' eggs fall off the rabbit's body and lie in the bedding and cracks in the hutch floor, sometimes for many months before hatching, the animal's housing should be cleaned thoroughly and treated with a special aerosol that destroys flea larvae in the environment and is effective for several months. This is available from your vet.

of cotton wool dampened in warm olive oil will help ear hygiene.

■ **Manges** of all types are caused by tiny mites which damage the skin. They are easily killed by modern anti-parasitic preparations, but wherever skin disease is diagnosed, you must be sure to isolate the patient from other rabbits and to clean and disinfect the hutch and run thoroughly.

Treatment The vet may give you some form of medicated bath with which to treat your rabbit if the body is affected. There is no harm in bathing a rabbit provided you use warm water and then dry your pet thoroughly with a soft towel and/or a hair-dryer. For localized problems, special aerosols are sometimes used. Drops are used in the ears.

■ **Lumps and bumps** If your rabbit develops one or more bumps under the skin, don't panic about myxomatosis. Other things are far more likely to be the cause. Sometimes a swelling will come up on the jaw or there may be several distributed irregularly over the head and body. Often there is no loss of appetite, at least at first, and the general condition of the animal seems normal. Abscesses, caused by various types of bacteria which arrive either through the bloodstream or via a bite wound, are commonly the cause. Sometimes the bug involved is the one that causes 'foot-rot' in sheep and which lives normally in the skin of the healthy rabbit. Occasionally lumps are tumours. Most are operable if caught early.

Note: all bumps need veterinary attention. Some may need lancing or removal under local anaesthetic or freezing spray, and usually the vet will also give an injection of an appropriate antibiotic. Seek advice early.

■ Miscellaneous ailments

■ Middle ear disease

If a rabbit starts to tilt its head to one side and, later, develop a tendency to move in circles, it may have infection of the middle ear. This disease is normally associated with a recent attack of 'snuffles', perhaps one as mild as merely a runny nose and watery eyes. The Pasteurella bacterium is the usual cause and treatment may have to be a prolonged course of broad-spectrum antibiotics. Chronic cases, particularly where the inner ear is also affected, can be very difficult to resolve.

■ Eye problems

The commonest eye troubles are runny, 'mattery', perhaps blood-shot eyes on one or both sides. The cause may be a mild injury, a fly-born infection or the presence of 'snuffles'.

Treatment Wash the eye carefully with warm water containing a little salt, wiping away any crusting around the eyelids, and apply Golden Eye ointment, which is obtainable from the pharmacist. If the condition persists for more than forty-eight hours, consult your vet. Antibiotic eye preparations may be indicated.

■ Mastitis inflammation

This, with swelling and tenderness of a doe's breast tissue, usually

Less common diseases

There are numerous other, though generally less common, diseases of rabbits. Even appendicitis can occur, the rabbit being one of the few animals other than man to have an appendix.

■ Within the last ten years, another new disease of rabbits, rabbit haemorrhagic virus or rabbit calicivirus, has spread from China into Europe and Central America. Again, domestic rabbits in contact directly or indirectly with wild rabbits are at risk. The good news is that a protective vaccine is available against this plague which can kill rabbits in as little as two days.

indicates the presence of mastitis. It tends to occur where management is lax and when the offspring are suddenly weaned or removed at, say, three to four weeks rather than the usual seven to eight weeks.

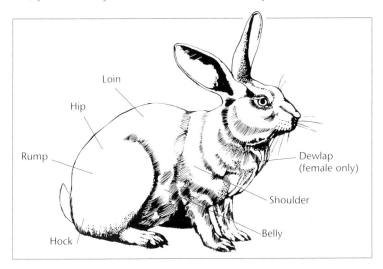 **Treatment** Bathe the swollen breasts frequently with warm water and seek veterinary attention. Broad-spectrum antibiotics are usually required.

■ Paralysis

Loss of function, paralysis, of the hind parts can be due to violent struggling during handling or some other form of injury. It is a very serious condition needing immediate veterinary attention which usually includes X-raying. Medical treatment is helpful in a minority of cases, but if there is not the first evidence of significant improvement within three weeks of onset, the outlook is bleak.

■ Summary

However, if you purchase good stock, provide good housing, maintain a regular cleaning routine and feed your pet an adequate balanced diet, you will find your visits to the vet will be very rare indeed.

Loin
Hip
Rump
Hock
Dewlap
(female only)
Shoulder
Belly

Guinea pigs

Guinea pigs fall ill from time to time, particularly if overcrowded or kept in unhygienic conditions. Germs and parasites build up in the environment and the result is outbreaks of diarrhoea, pneumonia, colds, weakness and weight loss, sometimes rapidly fatal. Food and bedding contaminated by the urine and droppings of wild rodents may bring in serious infections such as salmonellosis.

■ Seek veterinary help

If a guinea pig falls ill, take it to the vet straightaway; diagnosis, sometimes aided by laboratory tests, will be followed by treatment either by injection or by the prescription of soluble drugs to be added to the water container. The vet won't normally use penicillin on guinea pigs; curiously, it is poisonous for these creatures. Other antibiotics thought to be dangerous for guinea pigs are bacitracin, ampicillin, streptomycin, lincomycin, erythromycin and tetracycline.

■ Tooth troubles
As for rabbits
(see page 106).

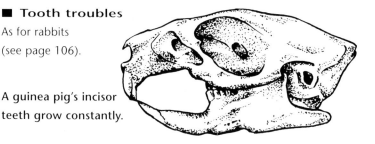

A guinea pig's incisor
teeth grow constantly.

■ Overgrown claws

Trimming a guinea pig's overgrown claws is best done by a veterinary surgeon. However, if you feel competent to perform this task, refer to page 108 and follow the same procedure as for rabbits.

Fleas

Very occasionally guinea pigs do get fleas. If you suspect that your animal is infested, then turn to page 110 and treat as for rabbits.

■ Diarrhoea

Similar diseases to those in rabbits (see page 107) occur in guinea pigs. Also they have a tendency to develop pseudotuberculosis, a bacterial disease, which often produces diarrhoea and weight loss with death after two to four weeks. An acute form that leads to blood poisoning and death within one to two days also exists. Such cases require urgent veterinary consultation. Diarrhoea in guinea pigs is also sometimes due to diet changes or environmental stress; certain antibiotics can cause diarrhoea and a fatal enteritis in these animals.

■ Skin disease

This is commonly caused by lice or mites and can be controlled by insecticide aerosols or powders obtained from the pet shop, together with disposal of all bedding and disinfection of the animals' living quarters. Stubborn skin disease may be due to other causes, such as fungus, and needs veterinary attention.

■ Guinea pigs sometimes chew the hair off themselves or one another ('barbering'). In such cases, it can help to change the housing or, at least, the bedding materials. Baldness is commonly seen in heavily pregnant sows – the cause is not known but the hair normally grows back after they give birth.

■ Feet

As in rabbits, rough damp or dirty flooring can result in guinea-pigs' feet becoming inflamed and even ulcerated. Softer bedding and a change of flooring is indicated, but take the animal to a vet who may treat the sore feet with antibiotics and corticosteroids. Healing often takes a very long time.

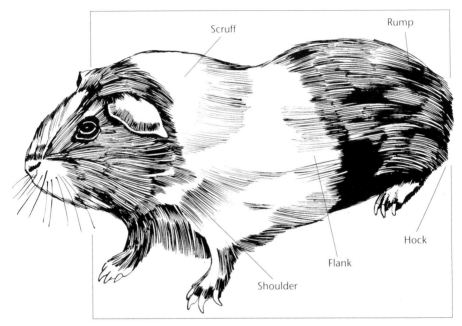

Scruff

Rump

Hock

Flank

Shoulder

■ Lumps and bumps

Many of these that you come across in or under the skin are often abscesses or infected lymph nodes ('glands'). They require veterinary treatment as for rabbits (see page 111).

■ Other ailments

Problems during pregnancy, and difficult births, which sometimes terminate in death during labour, are quite common. Try to avoid waiting any longer than when the sow is four months old when mating her for the first time (see page 87). Troubles during pregnancy are often the result of feeding hay of poor quality. Plenty of roughage in the form of top-quality hay is absolutely essential.

■ Pregnancy toxaemia

This disease develops during the last one to two weeks of pregnancy or the first five days after giving birth. The sow is off her food, depressed and may breathe heavily. Fat animals are more susceptible so avoid over-feeding. This disease progresses rapidly, is difficult to treat and frequently ends in death. Veterinary attention at the first sign of trouble is essential.

■ Mastitis
As for rabbits (see page 112).

■ Eye troubles
As for rabbits (see page112).

■ Vitamin C deficiency ('scurvy')
Guinea pigs need lots of Vitamin C regularly. If they don't get enough they lose weight and condition, their limb joints become enlarged and painful (due to internal haemorrhages), they are weak and lame and eventually they die. Symptoms can occur as early as two weeks after a shortage of Vitamin C begins.

Treatment This consists of giving 100 mg Vitamin C (ascorbic acid) by drops into the mouth once a day.

Causes of disease

■ The major group of illnesses in guinea pigs are caused by dietary faults. Shortage of good hay can produce 'barbering', death of youngsters, loss of condition, overgrowth of teeth with resultant difficulties in eating, and self-mutilation. Ill-balanced diets may lead to bone disease. Mouldy vegetable food may produce serious liver damage, enteritis and a high mortality rate.

■ If one among a group of animals dies, it is wise to have a post-mortem examination carried out. Accurate diagnosis enables you to take swift action, perhaps by adding drugs to the water or food, to protect the living.

Hamsters

Hamsters are tougher and less often laid up than other domesticated rodents, but they have their special problems.

Scruff   Shoulder   Flank   Rump

■ The mouth

■ **Tooth problems** can occur as with rabbits (see page 106). Overgrown teeth, caused usually by the diet not demanding sufficient chewing, may need clipping and rasping back by a vet. Feeding too many sweet 'treats' and household titbits can, as in children, lead to caries (cavities) in the teeth.

■ **Sticky 'treats'**, such as toffees, occasionally become jammed in the hamster's cheek pouches which have a dry lining normally. A vet will flush out the pouches.

■ Tummy troubles

Diarrhoea can be caused by a variety of germs and other factors.

■ Contamination of food or bedding with germs of the ubiquitous Salmonella group is a constant risk to hamsters. The commonest source of these bugs is wild mouse or rat droppings. Symptoms may be vague: dullness, lack of appetite and diarrhoea. Death may ensue quickly. Only speedy treatment by a vet, who will inject a tiny quantity of special antibiotic into the hamster, can save the day.

Certain antibiotics are thought to be toxic to hamsters. They include penicillin, streptomycin, lincomycin and erythromycin.

■ Wet tail

The nuisance disease of hamsters is undoubtedly 'wet tail'. This persistent and weakening diarrhoea is due to a gastro-intestinal upset whose causes seem to be complex. Too much fat in the diet, vitamin deficiency (particularly of the vitamin B group), stress and several kinds of bacteria have all been blamed at different times.

Treatment This involves improving the patient's eating habits and living conditions, adding a little yeast to the food and often, under veterinary advice, putting an antibiotic, such as soluble neomycin, in the drinking water.

■ Tyzzer's disease

This may also affect hamsters (see rabbits, page 107).

■ Constipation

This is often seen in young hamsters who are just beginning to wean and where only dry food is available. They must be able to reach a supply of water at all times. Constipated hamsters are miserable, exhibit swollen abdomens and frequently bulging anuses. Use 'Micralax' enemas and provide milk 'pobs', oatmeal porridge, fresh greens and soft fruit.

■ Coughs, sneezes and snuffles

Hamsters can pick up some of the cold sore-throat viruses of humans, so don't let folk afflicted in this way handle or come near your pets. Virus infections contracted from humans can progress to pneumonia and may prove fatal.

Treatment Sneezing, snuffles and sore noses in hamsters are signs of respiratory infection. As with humans, good nursing may be all that is required – warmth, swabbing away nasal discharges, vitamin supplements etc. In more severe cases, a vet may prescribe an antibiotic to ward off potentially dangerous secondary infections by bacteria such as Pasteurella.

■ Skin disease

This can be due to fungus (ringworm), mites (mange), infection of bite wounds or degeneration due to old age. Often owners mistake two patches of dark coarse hair, one on each side over the hips, for skin disease. Actually these patches, more obvious in males than in females, are normal and are the sites of special glands. These glands play a part in sexual attraction (hamsters in the wild seek out their mates by smell) and are possibly also used for marking out territory.

Diagnosis and treatment The vet will diagnose the type of any skin ailment, often with the aid of laboratory tests on skin or hair scrapings, and then prescribe specific treatment.

Other ailments

■ 'Cage paralysis', where a hamster seems to become very weak on its legs, is due to lack of space and exercise. The owner must speedily provide both, not least by installing a good exercise wheel.

■ Pregnancy toxaemia can occur as in guinea pigs (see page 116).

■ Diabetes of hereditary origin is sometimes detected by the vet where an animal drinks copiously. Such a patient may lose much weight or, alternatively, be obese.

■ Tumours, particularly inoperable ones of the adrenal gland, are found in around fifty per cent of hamsters over two years of age.

Note: besides the above-mentioned antibiotics, certain other chemicals are toxic for hamsters. Among them are DDT and organo-phosphorous compounds (used in some insecticides and parasiticides).

■ Gerbils

■ Tooth trouble

Like the other small pets, gerbils may have to have their front teeth trimmed back if they overgrow. The cause of such exuberant growth is deformities of the mouth structures or, more commonly, nothing to gnaw on in their cage.

■ Diarrhoea

'Wet tail' and Salmonellosis occur as in hamsters (see page 118). The causes and treatment are the same. The most serious disease of gerbils, often, but not always, causing diarrhoea, along with depression, lack of appetite and weight loss, is Tyzzer's disease (see rabbits, page 107). Sometimes it attacks so ferociously that the victims are simply found dead. This disease may prove rapidly fatal (within two days of the onset of symptoms) in up to seventy per cent of cases. Treatment is difficult and depends on rapid veterinary attention, fluid therapy, good nursing and the use of antibiotics such as oxytetracycline and neomycin.

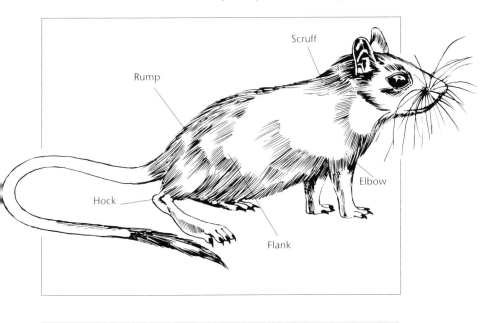

Scruff

Rump

Elbow

Hock

Flank

Diarrhoea in gerbils can often be the result of poor feeding, particularly spoiled or stale food or an excess of wet greens. To avoid this, make sure you feed your pet correctly (see page 77 for the basic guidelines to a balanced diet).

■ 'Colds'

Sneezes, snuffles and sore eyes are frequently the result of streptococcal bacteria picked up from children. Antibiotics are the best treatment.

■ Skin disease

As for rabbits (see page 109).

■ Other ailments

■ Infected sebaceous gland

The large sebaceous gland located under the belly of gerbils sometimes becomes infected, inflamed and swollen. The vet will prescribe a suitable antibiotic/corticosteroid ointment with which to anoint the sore areas.

■ **Tumours,** some of which are operable, are common in gerbils. The commonest organs to be affected by tumours are the ovaries and uterus.

■ **Note:** some 'narrow-spectrum' antibiotics, such as penicillin and streptomycin, can cause dangerous after-effects in gerbils. Only 'broad-spectrum' antibiotics, such as chloramphenicol, tetracyclines and cephalosporins, will be prescribed for them by the vet.

Rats and mice

If you clean out your pets' cages conscientiously and provide wholesome food and clean water regularly, illness should rarely be seen. Rodents can be affected by a large number of ailments, but these are most often encountered in the large colonies kept by laboratories. If your pet does become ill, take him along to your vet. He can give minute injections if necessary or prescribe medicine to be added to the water bottle.

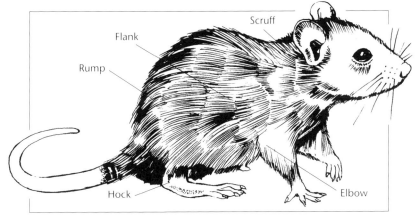

Scruff

Flank

Rump

Hock

Elbow

■ Tooth troubles

As with the other small rodents, overgrowth of the gnawing incisor teeth may result in poor appetite and loss of weight. If it occurs, you can carefully trim back the teeth to their normal length using nail clippers.

■ Stomach upsets

All the causes described for rabbits and the other rodents can produce diarrhoea and digestive upsets in rats and mice, including Tyzzer's disease.

■ **Parasitic worms**, both tapeworms and roundworms, occasionally cause diarrhoea, loss of condition, loss of weight and, less frequently, rectal prolapse. The presence of worms is easily confirmed by laboratory testing of droppings, and treatment consists of the administration of safe drugs such as mebendazole in food or water. First aid for simple diarrhoea is the administration of Kaopectate suspension (available from a pharmacist without prescription). The dose is 0.5 ml daily for a rat and 0.1 ml daily for a mouse, in two divided doses given orally by an eye-dropper or small syringe.

■ Chest troubles

'Colds', heavy breathing, wheezing and runny noses, often accompanied by weight loss and dullness, are signs of respiratory disease – probably the commonest type of sickness in rats and mice. Although viruses and bacteria of many kinds are the causal agents of the disease, other factors such as poor housing, bad hygiene and overcrowding play an important part in predisposing the animals to germ attack. Antibiotics in the water supply may be used to treat such conditions, but prevention in the form of improved housing and management is the watchword.

■ Skin disease

The diseases of the skin affecting rats and mice are those described in the rabbit (page 109) and other small pets.

■ **Skin abscesses** caused by bites when fighting are often seen. Don't keep male mice together – they are likely to do battle.

■ Other ailments

Diseases of the nervous system are common in rats and mice but are not treatable and are mainly of interest only to laboratory scientists. Certain antibiotics, such as penicillin and streptomycin, can be toxic to rats and mice. Your vet has others he can use safely.

■ Tumours, especially of the breast tissue, are sometimes seen in these animals. In rats they are usually benign whereas in mice they tend to be malignant. It is feasible for a vet to operate, under general anaesthetic, and remove the benign sort of tumour.

First aid for the small pet

Small pets need expert attention in most cases when they fall ill or have an accident. Disease can proceed rapidly, sometimes to a fatal conclusion, and you should never waste time on patent remedies and experiments. In general, owners can do far less for the small pet in trouble than for bigger animals such as cats and dogs. Diagnosis and advice from a veterinary surgeon must always be sought without delay.

■ Fractures

Where it is suspected that fractures may have been caused by a fall or other trauma, do not attempt to splint the animal's legs with matchsticks or the like. Manipulating the delicate limbs can easily cause further serious damage to fine nerves and blood vessels. Instead, pick the animal up by its scruff (see pages 41-43), wrap it gently in some soft material, keep it warm and take it to the vet's surgery or local animal clinic immediately. Offering or administering by dropper some warm, sweetened water to avoid dehydration can be beneficial, but do not feed the animal – it may have to be anaesthetized.

■ Small cuts and wounds

These can be bathed gently in warm water and very weak antiseptic, and then dried. A tiny amount of antiseptic or antibiotic cream can then be applied to the cut or wound. However, powders are best avoided on hairy parts of the body as they tend to create matting.

Holidays

What should you do when you go away? Of course, you must NEVER even contemplate simply piling a vast quantity of food and water into the animal's quarters and hoping it will work its way through them and even have some left over by the time you return sunburnt and laden with duty-frees.

■ The best thing you can do is to arrange for a friend to visit the house at least once a day to feed and water your pets, and, as necessary, clean them out.

■ Written instructions should be left and are better than verbal ones which can be forgotten easily.

■ Another way is to board out your pet, preferably together with its own familiar accommodation, at a friend's house or at a pet shop, boarding kennels (some of these are prepared to 'put up' small pets nowadays), an RSPCA clinic or veterinary surgery.

■ Again, make sure that you take along some notes on the animal's usual diet and a pack or two of its brand of food, so that the risk of nutritional upset is minimized. Even mice can suffer from 'holiday tummy'.

Summary

So now we come to the end of this little instruction manual for owners of small pets. Good luck with your small-pet-keeping, but please, if you are unable to devote regular time and care to the servicing and maintenance of your beast, stick to train-spotting or whatever your particular hobby may be. Only good owners are welcome in this club!

Index

Abscesses, 124
Abyssinian guinea pigs, 27
Angora rabbits, 13, 16
  grooming, 98
Appendicitis, 112
Bamboo rats, 36
'Barbering', 105
Bedding,
  for gerbils, 61, 92
  for guinea pigs, 56
  for hamsters, 59
  for rabbits, 51
Belgian hares, 16
Birch mice, 34
Birth,
  of gerbils, 92
  of hamsters, 90
  of rabbits, 85
Breathing, heavy, 124
Breeding, 81-96
  and diet, 79
  gerbils, 91-93
  guinea pigs, 87-88
  hamsters, 89-90
  mice, 94-96
  rabbits, 81-86
  rats, 94-96
Brewer's yeast, 76
Buying a small pet, 39-40
  breeders, 40
  gerbils, 48
  guinea pigs, 46
  hamsters, 47
  hobbyists, 40
  mice, 48
  pet shops, 40
  rabbits, 44-45
  rats, 48
Cages,

for gerbils, 61
for guinea pigs, 55
for hamsters, 57-58
hygiene, 97
for mice, 61-62
for rats, 62-63
Calcium caseinate, 86
Capromys, 36
Capybaras, 24
Chinchillas, 14
Claws, overgrown, 108, 114
Climbing devices, 66-67
Coccidiosis, 69, 105
Colds, 122, 124
Coneys, 16
Constipation, 106, 119
Coughs, 119
Courtship displays, 88
Deer mice, 35
Dental problems, 106, 118, 121, 123
Diabetes, 120
Diarrhoea, 78, 105, 107, 114, 115, 118-119, 121, 123
Distress, in rodents, 97
Drinking utensils, 65
  hygiene of, 98
Dust baths, 67
Dutch rabbits, 15, 16
Ear(s), 110-111
  canker, 110-111
  middle ear disease, 111-112
Eczema, 'wet', 110
English guinea pigs, 27
English rabbits, 16
Exercise, 52, 65-66
  runs, 52, 56, 65-66
  wheels, 59, 67

Eye problems, 112, 117
First aid, 125
Fleas, 110, 115
Flemish Giants, 16
Food,
  for gerbils, 77-78
  pregnant, 92
  for guinea pigs, 74-75
  for hamsters, 76
  for mice, 79-80
  pots, 64-65, 98
  for rabbits, 68-73
  pregnant, 85
  for rats, 79-80
Foot problems, 115
Formula milk, 86
Fractures, 125
Fur balls, 105
Gas, 107
Gerbils, 31-33
  breeding, 91-93
  choosing, 48
  feeding, 77-78
  handling, 43
  illnesses of, 121-122
  Mongolian, 31, 77
  pregnancy in, 92
  sexing, 101
  Wagner's, 32
Gnawing logs, 53, 63, 66
Grasshopper mice, 34
Grooming, 98
Guinea pigs, 25-28
  Abyssinian, 27
  breeding, 87-88
  choosing, 46
  English, 27
  feeding, 74-75
  handling, 42
  housing, 54-56

illnesses of, 114-117
  mating, 87-88
  Peruvian, 27
  sexing, 102
Hamsters, 29-30
  breeding, 89-90
  Chinese, 29
  choosing, 47
  European, 29
  feeding, 76
  golden, 29
  handling, 42
  housing, 57-59
  pregnancy in, 90
  sexing, 101
Handling, 41-43
  gerbils, 43
  guinea pigs, 42
  hamsters, 42
  mice, 43
  rabbits, 41
  rats, 43
Hares, 8, 9, 10
  Belgian, 16
Harlequin rabbits, 16
Havana rabbits, 14
Hay, 65, 70, 74, 75, 116
  racks, 65
Himalayan rabbits, 16, 22
Holidays, 126
Hooded rats, 35
Housing, 49-63
  gerbils, 60-61
  guinea pigs, 54-56
  mice, 61-62
  rabbits, 49-52
  rats, 62-63
Humidity, 59
Hutches,
  for guinea pigs, 54

hygiene of, 97
for rabbits, 49-52, 104
for rats, 63
Hygiene, 97-98
Illnesses,
of gerbils, 121-122
of guinea pigs, 114-117
of hamsters, 118-120
of mice, 123-124
of rabbits, 103-113
of rats, 123-124
Jerboa rats, 36
Jumping mice, 34
Lactation, 69, 84-86
Lagomorphs, 8, 9, 16
Lop rabbits, 16
Mallomys, 36
Mange, 109-110, 111, 120
Mastitis, 112-113, 117
Mating,
in gerbils, 91
in guinea pigs, 87-88
in hamsters, 89-90
in rabbits, 81-83
Mice, 34-36
breeding, 94-96
choosing, 48
feeding, 79-80
handling, 43
housing, 61-62
illnesses of, 123-124
sexing, 102
Middle ear disease, 111-112
Mineral lick blocks, 73
Mites, 120
Mongolian gerbils, 77
Mucoid enteritis, 108
Myxomatosis, 103-104, 111
Nervous system diseases, 124
Nesolagus, 13

Nesting boxes, 65, 92
Netherland Dwarf rabbits, 16
New Zealand rabbits, 14
Oestrus, 88, 92
Old English rabbits, 15, 23
Oryctolagus, 12
Outdoor runs, 52-53, 56
Paralysis, 113
cage, 120
Parasitic worms, 123
Pens, 55
Pentalagus, 12
Peruvian guinea pigs, 27, 98
Pikas, 9
Pneumonia, 114
Poisonous plants, 72
Pregnancy,
diet in, 92
false, 83, 90, 92
feeding in, 69
in gerbils, 92
in guinea pigs, 88, 116-117
in hamsters, 90
in mice, 94, 96
in rabbits, 83
in rats, 94, 96
Pronolagus, 17
Rabbits, 8-23
breeding, 81-86
choosing, 44-45
digestion of, 20-21
feeding, 68-73
fur, 22
handling, 41
hearing, 20
housing, 49-52
illnesses of, 103-113
kittens, development of, 85-86
mating, 81-83

pregnancy in, 83
reproductive life of, 86
sexing, 99
species, 12-16
weight of, 16-17
Rats, 36-38
breeding, 94-96
choosing, 48
feeding, 79-80
handling, 43
housing, 62-63
illnesses of, 123-124
sexing, 102
sight of, 37
water requirements of, 37-38
Rectal prolapse, 123
Refection, 21
Rex rabbits, 14
Ringworm, 109-110, 120
Rodents, 8, 24-38
gerbils, 31-33
guinea pigs, 25-28
hamsters, 29-30
mice, 34-36
rats, 36-38
Roundworms, 123
Sable rabbits, 14
Salmonella infection, 108
Salmonellosis, 114
Satin rabbits, 14
Scurvy, 117
Sebaceous gland, infected, 122
Selevin's mouse, 35
Sexing, 98
gerbils, 101
guinea pigs, 100
hamsters, 101
mice, 102
rabbits, 99
rats, 102
Skin disease, 109, 115,

120, 122, 124
Smoke pearl rabbits, 14
Sneezes, 119, 122
Snuffles, 108, 119, 122
Spiny pocket mice, 34
Swarth's rice rat, 37
Syphilis, rabbit, 109
Syrian hamsters, 29
Tapeworm(s), 123
cysts, 105
Teeth, 20-21, 28, 106, 114
dental problems, 106, 118, 121, 123
disease of, 72
Temperature, taking, 109
Temperature range,
for gerbils, 61
for guinea pigs, 54
for hamsters, 58
for mice, 62
for rabbits, 51
for rats, 63
Toxaemia, pregnancy, 116-117, 120
Toys, 67
Treadmill wheels, 67
Tumours, 120, 122, 124
Tyzzer's disease, 107, 119, 121, 123
Vitamins and minerals, 73, 74, 75
deficiencies, 117, 119
Water, 71, 75, 80
containers, 64, 65
rats, 36
Weaning, 93
Weight, loss of, 105, 114, 123
'Wet eczema', 110
'Wet tail', 76, 119
Wheezing, 124
Wood logs, 53, 63, 66
Wounds, 125